# Malachi: Rekindling the Fires of Faith

Page H. Kelley

Convention Press • Nashville, Tennessee

# CONTENTS

1. How Have You Loved Us? (1:1-5) .................... 4

2. How Have We Despised Your Name? (1:6 to 2:9) ...... 20

3. Why Are We Faithless to One Another? (2:10-16) ..... 39

4. Where Is the God of Justice? (2:17 to 3:5) ............ 67

5. How Shall We Return? (3:6-12) ....................... 91

6. What Is the Good of Keeping His Charge? (3:13 to 4:6) .................................... 110

The Church Study Course .......................... 125

How to Request Credit for This Course .............. 127


5132-36

This book is the text for a course in the subject area Bible Study of the Church Study Course.

Target group: This book is designed for adults and is part of the Church Study Course Offerings. The 1963 statement of "The Baptist Faith and Message" is the doctrinal guideline for the writer and editor.

Dewey Decimal Classification Number: 224.99
Subject Heading: Bible O. T. Malachi
Printed in the United States of America.

# A WORD TO BEGIN . . .

The fact that the Book of Malachi is placed last in the Old Testament in English Bibles may be symbolic of the place it occupies in many people's thinking. Largely, it is viewed as a minor book among the Minor Prophets. It is known primarily for its passage on tithing. In addition, some interpreters have charged that the prophet Malachi was a rigid legalist. These people point to Malachi's emphasis on sacrificial rites and tithing, and his injunction to "'remember the law of . . . Moses'" (4:4). However, a serious study of Malachi's book shows that he stressed the inwardness of a genuine religion that affected all of life—a walking with God "'in peace and uprightness'" (2:6). Malachi was a courageous, innovative voice crying in a wilderness of religious apathy and doubt. He deserves more attention and respect than we have given him. This textbook introduces us—or reintroduces us—to the neglected riches in the Book of Malachi.

The writer of the textbook is Page H. Kelley, John R. Sampey Professor of Old Testament Interpretation at The Southern Baptist Theological Seminary, Louisville, Kentucky. Dr. Kelley makes the Book of Malachi come alive with fresh words from God for our day.

The textbook may be used in personal or group study. In both uses, the Personal Learning Activities at the end of each chapter will help the learner to review the material that has been covered. The companion Study Guide will provide helpful resources for the teacher and the members. The Teaching Guide will aid the teacher in directing the study. The *Teaching Resource Kit for Malachi: Rekindling the Fires of Faith, 1988* contains visuals and other materials that will help the teacher in guiding the study. In this textbook, guidance for using Personal Learning Activities is in the section entitled "The Church Study Course" at the end of the book.

Also at the back of the book is a Church Study Course Credit request (Form 725). On completing this book, the pupil should mail the completed form to the indicated address.

Eli Landrum, Jr., editor

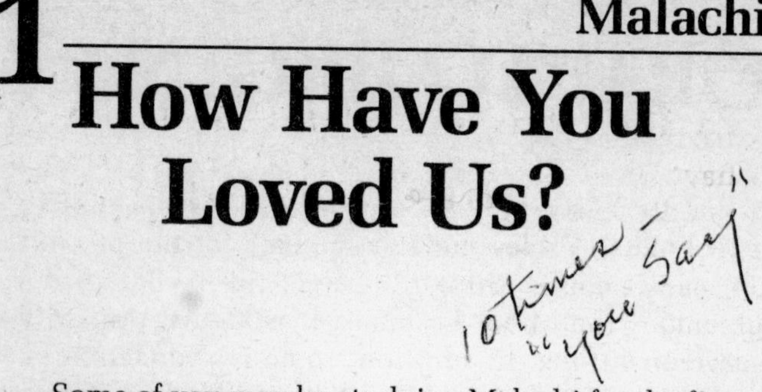

# 1 How Have You Loved Us?

## Malachi 1:1-5

Some of you may be studying Malachi for the first time. If so, you are about to meet one of the Old Testament's most fearless and hard-hitting prophets. While he is counted among the twelve so-called "minor prophets," certainly nothing is minor about his message. He probably was called to minister in the middle of the fifth century BC, at a time when Israel's existence was hanging in the balance. The fact that the nation survived the crisis was due in no small part to his courageous efforts.

Malachi has been called "the Hebrew Socrates," since both he and the famous Greek philosopher taught the people by engaging them in conversation or dialogue. To be sure, he did not learn his dialogical style from Socrates but from the prophets who preceded him. The Old Testament records other instances where the people's words, spoken in a spirit of arrogance and disdain for God, were used to frame God's indictment of them. (See Pss. 10:4,6; 11,13; 14:1; Isa. 28:14-18; Jer. 2:23,25,35.) This was a case of the people being condemned out of their own mouths.

Malachi seized the conversation technique of preaching and developed it to perfection. Whereas the former prophets had used it only occasionally, he employed it almost exclusively as the vehicle of God's message to a stubborn and rebellious people. Each of the six main divisions in the book (1:1-5; 1:6 to 2:9; 2:10-16; 2:17 to 3:5; 3:6-12; 3:13 to 4:6) includes three subdivisions: *(a)* the statement of a charge or proposition; *(b)* the people's flat denial of the charge or proposition; and *(c)* the marshalling of evidence that could not be denied to support the charge or proposition.

Of particular significance in Malachi's pattern of presentation are the people's responses to God's charges and propositions. Their defiant attitude reflected the essence of their sin and the defection from which they had to return to God. They constantly mocked God by hurling His words back in His face:

"'How hast thou loved us?'" (1:2).
"'How have we despised thy name?'" (1:6).
"'How have we polluted it [the altar]?'" (1:7).
"'Why does he not [accept our offering]?'" (2:14).
"'How have we wearied him?'" (2:17).
"'How shall we return?'" (3:7).
"'How are we robbing thee?'" (3:8).
"'How have we spoken against thee?'" (3:13).[1]

The people's questions became more and more defiant until the Lord was forced to say, "'Your words have been stout against me'" (3:13), or as *The New English Bible* renders: "You have used hard words about me."[2] In a real sense, the people had called down punishment on their own heads.

Now, turn to the first division of Malachi, 1:1-5. The proposition that the Lord stated was: "'I have loved you'" (1:2). The doubting congregation's response was: "'How hast thou loved us?'" (1:2).

The first division of Malachi sets the stage for the entire book. God's steadfast love for His people was in stark contrast to their indifference, cynicism, and open contempt for Him. He had gone on being true to His covenant; they had gone on ignoring and breaking it. He who was great "'beyond the border of Israel'" (v. 5) merited their love, reverence, and obedience. The prophet came on the scene to remind them of their duty. His task was to rekindle fires of faith that almost had gone out.

## Malachi, the Lord's Messenger (1:1)

### An Ominous Message

The term used to describe the word of the Lord addressed to Israel through Malachi is **oracle** (1:1). Sometimes, this term also is rendered *burden*, since its root meaning is *to lift up* or *to bear*. The verb root may be used of a person lifting up his or her voice in order to speak (Num. 23:7), to weep (Gen. 27:38), or to sing (Isa. 24:14).

Whenever "oracle" is used to designate a prophetic utterance, it always is an utterance that is threatening and condemnatory in character. T. V. Moore described the threatening nature of such oracles: "Like some dark cloud, heavy with its pent-up fury, these prophecies are surcharged with the wrath of God, and hang ready to pour their dreadful contents on those against whom they are directed."[3] In order to reflect the threatening nature of Malachi's message, one might render the title verse: The awesome revelation of the word of the Lord to Israel by the hand of Malachi. Malachi's words were addressed to Israel, the generally accepted designation for the entire remnant of the Jewish nation in the period after the Exile. Israel was synonymous with God's covenant people. Every indication is that Malachi was a citizen of Jerusalem and that Jerusalem was the scene of most, if not all, of his preaching.

**The Messenger**

Who was Malachi? Many interpreters have agreed that in its Hebrew form, *Malachi* is a title and not a personal name. As a title, **Malachi** literally means *my angel* or *my messenger*. This identical form appears also in 3:1, where it always is rendered as a title, "my messenger," and never as a proper name, "Malachi." The Septuagint, the Greek version of the Old Testament, translates 1:1 and 3:1 alike; in each instance, reference is made to the prophet as the Lord's "messenger."

The Targum of Jonathan, an ancient Aramaic version of the prophets, identified the author of the book as "Ezra the scribe." The Babylonian Talmud attributed the book to Mordecai. Other ancient proposals included Haggai, Zechariah, Zerubbabel, and Nehemiah. The Talmud took the position that the book was composed by "the men of the great synagogue." Among Christian scholars, Jerome and later Calvin supported the tradition that Ezra was the prophet and that Malachi was a title given to him. However, many interpreters hold that *Malachi* is a proper noun, a name.

Whoever he was, or whatever his name, he fully deserved to be called "the messenger of the Lord." Throughout this study, reference will be made to the prophet as Malachi.

**Dating Malachi's Ministry**

Scholars generally have agreed that Malachi should be dated 460-450 BC, near the time that Ezra and Nehemiah arrived in

Jerusalem. The fact that the Temple had been rebuilt and its services restored (see Mal. 1:7,10; 2:13; 3:1,10) demands a date after 516 BC, the date of the dedication of the new Temple. (See Ezra 6:14-15. Some scholars hold that the new Temple was completed in 515 BC.) Furthermore, the lack of zeal for the Temple and its services suggests a date considerably later than 516 BC.

One might say that Malachi fits the period of Ezra and Nehemiah like a bone fits its socket. Both Malachi and Nehemiah pictured Jerusalem as under the rule of a governor (Mal. 1:8; Neh. 5:15), which indicates that both belonged to the Persian period. Both described a situation in which the people had contempt for the Temple and disregard for its services (Mal. 1:7-14; 3:8-10; Neh. 13:10-12). Both blamed this sorry state of affairs on the priests (Mal. 2:8; Neh. 13:29). Malachi, Ezra, and Nehemiah wrestled with the problem of divorce and mixed marriages (Mal. 2:10-16; Ezra 9:1 to 10:44; Neh. 13:23-27).

Thus, the conclusion seems inevitable that Malachi was a contemporary of Ezra and Nehemiah. The view adopted in this textbook is that he preached in Jerusalem just prior to their arrival. He prepared the way for them.

**The Worst of Times**

About forty-two thousand Jews returned from Babylon in 538 BC. (See Ezra 2:64.) Soon, they set about rebuilding the Temple but were unable to continue because of the opposition of "the people of the land." (See Ezra 4:4-5.) Building was resumed in the second year of Darius (520 BC), and the Temple was dedicated four years later (around 516 BC). Inspiration for this undertaking was furnished by the prophets Haggai and Zechariah. (See Ezra 5:1-2; 6:14-15.)

The Old Testament account breaks off at this point, and the years from 516-460 BC are passed over in silence. This is one of the most obscure periods in Jewish history because it is less well documented than many earlier periods.

The silent period of 516-460 BC in Israel's history really was one of the decisive periods in world history. It was the period when the Greeks began to challenge the Persians for world supremacy. In 490 BC, under the leadership of Miltiades, the Greeks defeated the Persian army on the plains of Marathon.

Ten years later, they bravely withstood a Persian assault at Thermopylae and destroyed the Persian fleet at Salamis. This also was the period when Greece emerged as the world leader in the fields of literature, art, and philosophy. Pericles was born about 495 BC and Socrates about 470 BC. Therefore, that Malachi and Socrates were contemporaries is almost certain, although neither probably ever had heard of the other.

The decades just before 460 BC were some of the most difficult that the Jewish nation ever encountered. The Jews had returned from Babylon with the promises of the prophets ringing in their ears—promises of freedom, prosperity, and world dominion. (See Isa. 49:22-23; 54:1-3; 61:5-7.) When these promises were not fulfilled immediately, the prophets Haggai and Zechariah laid the blame on the people for not having rebuilt the Temple. (See Hag. 1:2-11.) Let this obstacle be removed, they said, and all of the promised blessings would be forthcoming. (See Hag. 2:6-9; Zech. 2:1-5; 8:1-8.) With their zeal rekindled by such assurances, the people set to work and completed the Temple in four years. Then, they waited for the Lord to perform His mighty acts on their behalf. But the years grew into decades, and nothing happened. Instead of becoming "a crown of beauty" and "a royal diadem" (Isa. 62:3), the people saw themselves as mere pawns in the Persians' hands.

The Persians ruled with an iron fist. They imposed a heavy tribute on the people and demanded that provisions be furnished for the soldiers who were quartered in the land. (See Neh. 5:15.) The Jews were not much better off under the Persians than they had been under the Babylonians. Poor economic conditions within the restored community added to the people's misery. Unemployment was widespread, for "there was no wage for man or any wage for beast" (Zech. 8:10). Crops failed because of droughts, plagues, and hailstorms. (See Hag. 1:10-11; 2:16-17.)

By Nehemiah's time, the situation had worsened. Many people were forced to mortgage their fields and houses and even to sell their children into slavery. (See Neh. 5:1-5.) The Temple offerings were diminished so greatly that the Levites and singers were forced to forsake the house of God and return to their fields in order to have food. (See Neh. 13:10-12; see also Mal. 3:8-10.) Most of the people experienced unrelieved poverty.

To make matters even worse, Jerusalem was surrounded by hostile foes. These included Samaritans, Arabians, Ammonites, Moabites, Edomites, and Philistines. They delayed the rebuilding of the Temple in the days of Zerubbabel. (See Ezra 4:4-5.) Later, they organized efforts to prevent Nehemiah's repairing the city's walls. (See Neh. 4:1-8; 6:1-9.) They made life miserable for the struggling community.

**A Dangerous Reaction**

Three-quarters of a century of hardship and disillusionment produced a dangerous reaction in Israel. The faith of former days gave way to doubt and skepticism. The people began to question whether the Lord loved them (Mal. 1:2). They even accused Him of showing preference toward evil persons and of failing to reveal Himself as the God of justice (2:17). They openly asserted that under His rule the wicked people fared better than the righteous persons (3:14-15). Thus, a new temper prevailed; and many became outright scoffers.

Three results of the decades of hardship and disillusionment may be noted. First, the people and the priests began to neglect the Temple and its services. They offered on the Lord's altar blemished and diseased animals (1:8,13-14). Tithes were kept for personal use instead of being brought to the Lord's storehouse (3:8-9). Such a mockery was made of worship that the Lord called for someone to close the Temple doors and to put out the altar fires (1:10).

Second, the Jews became less concerned about maintaining their distinct identity as God's covenant people. They began to intermarry with their heathen neighbors without considering the question of religion. It was a critical moment in the nation's struggle for survival. The distinctive Jewish institutions, especially the sabbath (see Neh. 13:15-22), were being threatened; and the Jews were in danger of being absorbed by their heathen neighbors.

Third, the nation's moral and ethical standards declined seriously. Money-lenders had no scruples against enslaving their own countrymen. (See Neh. 5:1-5.) Malachi charged the people with the sins of sorcery, adultery, perjury, and oppression of the community's defenseless members. (See 3:5.) He also described a situation in which brothers dealt treacherously with brothers (2:10), and the prevailing mood was one of alienation and distrust (4:6).

### A Faithful Remnant

The Jews' one source of hope in the crisis was a small band of devout believers who regarded the situation with growing alarm. They came together regularly to speak of the Lord's goodness and to give each other mutual support (3:16). They were the faithful remnant through which God's great purposes were to be realized.

Malachi's lot was to be the spokesman for the faithful group. Few prophets ever faced a more difficult situation. The age in which he lived was one of history's uneventful waiting periods when God seemed to have forgotten His people. Herein lies the prophet's significance for all times:

> Malachi's prophecy is particularly relevant to the many waiting periods in human history and in the lives of individuals. He enables us to see the strains and temptations of such times, the imperceptible abrasion of faith that ends in cynicism because it has lost touch with the living God. Even more important he shows the way back to a genuine, enduring faith in the God who does not change (Mal. 3:6), who invites men to return to Him (3:7), and never forgets those who respond (3:16).[4]

## A Loving Father and a Rebellious People (1:2-5)

### Love Declared and Denied (v. 2*a*)

In Malachi's day, religion seems to have been permeated by a spirit of trading. The people thought of God as a kind of heavenly broker who dispensed rewards and punishments in proportion to merit. When they felt that He had not taken sufficient notice of their merits, they lodged a "consumers' complaint" against Him. (See 3:14-15.)

Malachi's opening statement challenged the erroneous religious philosophy: "'I have loved you,' says the Lord" (v. 2). The love in view is described best as God's electing love. Such love was God's supreme gift to Israel, and it had been bestowed freely on Jacob and his descendants apart from any suggestion of merit. (See Deut. 7:6-8; 9:4-5.)

Over against God's declaration of love was Israel's denial of that love's reality. "'How hast thou loved us?'" is a rhetorical question. Its implied meaning is: *You haven't loved us at all!* The construction has the nature of a question and an exclamation, as if the people should be understood as saying: *Is that so?!*

**Proof of Divine Love (vv. 2*b*-5)**

As proof of His love for the people of Israel, the Lord cited His choice of their father Jacob over Esau. (See Gen. 25:21-23.) Malachi 1:2*b* leads into the subject of election, one of the most difficult subjects in the Bible.

How is one to interpret the passages that set forth Israel's special election to be God's covenant people? Some have regarded this teaching as nothing more than an expression of Jewish exclusiveness, an outgrowth of racial and religious pride. In response to this view, note that the record of slavery in Egypt, of deliverance at the Red Sea, and of constant rebellion in the wilderness is not the kind of record that a proud nation would have invented about itself. The Old Testament condemns religious and racial pride in no uncertain terms and constantly reminds Israel that the nation's election was not as much to privilege as to service.

God loved the Israelites simply because He chose to love them. The nation's election was rooted in divine love from beginning to end. The grounds for the choice lay in God alone and not in any special qualities that Israel had or any credits the nation had accumulated.

On the other hand, the purpose behind Israel's election is made clear. The nation was to be the pilot project in God's plan of redemption for all people. In choosing the Israelites, God sought to establish a beachhead in human history from which He would press His campaign until all nations acknowledged His sovereignty and submitted to His rule. (See Gen. 12:1-3.) Israel was elected primarily to mission and only secondarily to privilege. In God's kingdom, greatness always is based on service. (See Mark 10:42-54.)

*An Age-old Rivalry.*—God cited the devastation of the land of Edom as evidence of His love for Israel (Mal. 1:3). The Edomites were descendants of Esau, Jacob's twin brother. (See Gen. 25:19-26.) This meant that the Edomites and the Jews were blood brothers. In fact, the Edomites were the only people in antiquity with whom the Jews shared a common ancestry that involved both father and mother.

Few rivalries are as bitter as those between brothers, and the rivalry that began with Jacob and Esau was kept alive through their descendants. For the Israelites and the Edomites to live together peaceably proved impossible. Malachi 1:2-5 is only one of many Old Testament passages that condemn this ancient foe. Israel's hatred mounted to a white heat of helpless rage when the Edomites sided with the Babylonians during the final siege and destruction of Jerusalem in 587-586 BC.

When the Israelites forcibly were removed from their land and exiled to Babylon, the Edomites moved in and occupied the territory that lay south of Jerusalem. Some of the Edomites intermarried with the Israelites who were left in the region, and their offspring came to be known as Idumaeans. By a strange twist of fate, Palestine later came to be ruled by a king who traced his ancestry back to the Idumaeans: the despised Herod the Great.

The Jews hated the Edomites even more when the Jews returned from Exile and found the Edomites occupying part of their territory. For them to believe that even the Lord hated those who could act in such a dastardly way was easy. The Israelites never were able to recover the territory of Idumaea from Esau's descendants.

The devastation of Edom to which verse 3 refers was apparently fresh in the minds of Malachi's audience. Otherwise, it would have lost its force as proof of God's love for the Jews. The event cannot be identified with certainty. One suggestion is that the Babylonians may have launched an attack on Edom after their capture of Jerusalem in 587-586 BC, although the records of the period do not mention such an attack. In light of the fact that Edom was an ally of Babylon against Jerusalem, such an attack seems unlikely.

The more probable suggestion is that the devastation was caused by the Nabataeans, a group of desert tribesmen who may have begun to encroach on the territory of Edom as early as the sixth century BC. According to the Greek historian Diodorus, these invaders from the eastern desert eventually captured all of the territory of Edom, including the capital city of Petra. The Nabataeans raised Petra to its highest glory before they came under Roman control in AD 106. The ruins of Petra that many tourists see today are the Nabataean ruins.

*God's Hatred of Edom (vv. 3-4).*—How is the forthright statement that God hated Esau to be interpreted (v. 3)? Was Malachi merely reflecting his own hostile attitude toward this ancient foe? If so, it was not noble of him to attribute his own prejudice to God. Surely, a better explanation of Malachi's statement than this exists.

One suggestion for making God's declaration of hatred for Edom seem less harsh is to treat the words *to love* and *to hate* as relative terms. The first would mean *to love more*, the second *to love less*. Genesis 29:30-31 may lend support to this suggestion, for the statement that "Leah was hated" by Jacob (v. 31) is preceded by the statement that Jacob "loved Rachel more than Leah" (v. 30). A similar statement occurs in Deuteronomy 21:15-17, where rules of conduct were laid down for the man who had two wives, "one beloved, and another hated" (KJV). The context makes clear that this was the case of one wife being preferred over the other. Perhaps Jesus was using the same idiom when He said: "If any one comes to me and does not hate his own father and mother . . . he cannot be my disciple" (Luke 14:26); or, as Matthew reported: "He who loves father or mother more than me is not worthy of me" (Matt. 10:37*a*). In all of the examples cited, the one "loved" was placed in a primary position, while the one "hated" occupied a secondary position.

But is one justified in trying to soften the Lord's condemnation of Edom? One may argue that Malachi intended love to be regarded as the opposite of hatred. This would agree with the way these terms normally were used throughout the Old Testament. Regarding the statement that God hated Esau, one commentator has written: "Just as *I loved Jacob* is an expression of election, so this is an expression of rejection. Love and hate indicate decisive, uncompromising choice."[5]

The remainder of Malachi 1:3 supports the latter interpretation. It points to a recent destruction that laid waste the hill country of Edom and left it as a habitation of jackals. It suggests that Edom's devastated cities had become the haunts of wild-animal packs from the surrounding deserts. One visitor to Palestine has described such a scene: "Wherever the traveller camps in the Holy Land, he will nightly hear the wailing cry of the packs of jackals as they quarter the country in search of food . . . About the ruins of Baalbek the packs of jackals secrete themselves by hundreds: there their sudden howl would break the dead stillness of the night . . . till the air seemed filled as if with the wailing of a thousand infants."[6]

Edom's destruction is described not only as thorough but also as permanent. According to verse 4, the Edomites were boasting that they would build new cities on the ruins of the old ones. The Lord's response was framed in an emphatic form: "'*They* may build, *but I* will tear down.'" Apparently, they still exercised a measure of control over their affairs; but their situation was more shaky than they seem to have realized. Their destruction would become proverbial, and people would rename them "'the wicked country'" and "'the people with whom the Lord is angry for ever'" (v. 4*b*).

At an early stage in their history, the Edomites seem to have worshiped the same God as the Israelites, since God often is pictured as caring for them or even as coming forth from their territory. (See Deut. 2:4-5; 33:2; Judg. 5:4; Hab. 3:3.) Possibly, they later repudiated their allegiance to God; thus, like their forefather Esau, they despised their birthright. (See Gen. 25:29-34.) This may account for the strong language that Malachi used in condemning them.

The emphasis must be made that the primary purpose of verses 2-5 was not to condemn Edom. It was to reprimand the Jews for their indifference to and denial of the divine love.

*God's Greatness (v. 5).*—Malachi 1:1-5 concludes with what may have been a line from an ancient hymn. At the sight of Edom's devastated territory, the Israelites would begin to sing: *Great is the Lord above the territory of Israel. The Revised Standard Version* reads, "'Great is the Lord, beyond the border of Israel!'" This misses the author's intention. The same Hebrew word is translated "country" in verse 4 and "border" in verse 5.

*'I have laid waste his [Edom's] hill country'"* (Mal. 1:3).

In one instance, it refers to the whole territory of Edom and in the other instance to the whole territory of Israel. The word rendered "beyond" in verse 5 (RSV) normally means *over, above,* or *upon.* (See Gen. 1:7; Ezek. 1:26; Jonah 4:6.) Malachi was drawing a sharp contrast between the fate in store for the territory of Edom and God's intention for the territory of Israel. Edom would become a devastated and wicked territory; but Israel would become the territory over which God's sovereignty would be proclaimed.

The opening section of Malachi indicates two important things about God: (1) He is a God of love (v. 2); (2) He is a great God (v. 5). These truths belong together, for a divine love that was powerless would be as unthinkable as a divine power that was loveless. Malachi proclaimed a love that was all-powerful and a power that was all-loving.

## Malachi's Favorite Designation for God

Malachi's favorite designation for God was "Lord of hosts" (1:4). This title first occurs in the Old Testament in 1 Samuel 1:3, after which it occurs in 1 and 2 Samuel, 1 and 2 Kings, 1 and 2 Chronicles, Psalms, Isaiah, Jeremiah, and the Minor Prophets from Hosea through Malachi. The post-exilic prophets, including Malachi, employed this title with a frequency that was out of proportion to the size of their books.

The word for "hosts" ***(seba'oth)*** is used in several different ways in the Old Testament. It may refer to Israel's armies (1 Kings 2:5), to the sun, moon, and stars (Deut. 4:19), or to the angelic hosts of heaven (1 Kings 22:19). "Lord of hosts" seems to have originated in the time of the judges as a designation of the Lord as the commander of Israel's armies. Later, the meaning was expanded to include the hosts of heaven, astral as well as angelic. This title even appears in the Latin Vulgate as *Dominus Exercituum,* "Lord of armies." The Greek Septuagint, on the other hand, reads *Kurios Pantokratōr,* "Lord Almighty," a reading that has been adopted by the translation of *The New International Version.*[7] This Greek rendering also was brought over into the New Testament and lies behind such passages as 2 Corinthians 6:18 and Revelation 4:8. In two other New Testament passages (Rom. 9:29; Jas. 5:4), the Hebrew word for "hosts" ***(seba'oth)*** was brought into the Greek as ***sabaoth.*** This accounts for the unusual rendering, "Lord of Sabaoth," which appears in these two passages in the King James Version.

The widespread use of the title "Lord of Hosts" in exilic and post-exilic times raises an interesting question. If its primary meaning was "Lord of armies," why was it so popular at a time when Israel was ruled by foreigners and had no armies of its own? The answer seems to be that Israel's prophets used this designation for God when they wanted to rekindle hope in disillusioned hearts. Robert L. Ottley underscored this point when he noted that "Lord of hosts" was "'a name of memories and triumphs,' and perhaps came to be regarded as that title of Israel's God to which a ruined state or church might most fittingly appeal in times of national distress."[8] Malachi seems to have used the title in order to rekindle the fires of faith in a disillusioned people.

## Lessons for Life from Malachi 1:1-5

*New situations and new crises call for new approaches to ministry.*—In the Old Testament period, the mark of a true prophet was the ability to discern whether a given moment in history was under God's wrath or God's mercy. Malachi perceived that the times in which he lived called for a strong word of condemnation to a rebellious people. He also perceived that the old forms of speech were not adequate for the demands of his day. He clothed his message in a new form that was designed to speak more clearly and more forcefully.

Our time calls for new approaches to ministry. Let us be open to the Holy Spirit's leadership as we seek to address people on the run with a message that will make them stop and think. Seeking change merely for change's sake has no merit. But neither does opposing change have merit if such change opens the door to more effective ministry.

*The greatest single truth that we can learn from the Scriptures is that God loves us.*—Nothing we can do can cause Him to love us any more than He already does. He has loved us to the ultimate degree in Christ Jesus, and He whose essence is love could not love us more than that.

We do not have to earn God's love. He freely bestows it on us apart from any merit on our part. We have no claim on His love except our desperate need to be loved. He loves us, not because of who we are, but because of who He is. Such amazing grace should save us from despair and also from presumption. We cannot earn a salvation that is given so freely, and we certainly must not try to take credit for it. Spiritual pride is one of the most deadly sins that can afflict God's people. We need only to thank Him for His unspeakable gift.

*God's call to salvation is always a call to service.*—Service is not an elective but a requirement for Christians. The reason churches have full-time ministers is not that they might relieve the other members of their duty to minister but that they might equip all of the members for ministry. The world's needs are so great that they cannot be met unless all Christians are mobilized for the task.

*We should not be discouraged if we seem to be a small minority in the midst of a pagan environment.*—The Bible warns us that the way of salvation and discipleship never will be the way of the majority. (See Matt. 7:13-14.) Christian discipleship is far too costly to have mass appeal. (See Matt. 10:34-39.) Let us take care lest we cheapen the gospel's demands in order to secure a greater following. Jesus turned some "good" people away because they were not willing to go all the way with Him. (See Mark 10:17-22.) He was not interested in padding the rolls of His disciples.

*"Waiting periods" occur in history when God seems to have forgotten His people.*—Malachi ministered in such a period. God seemed to have forgotten the promises He had made to His people. Malachi called the people back to an enduring faith in the God who does not change, who invites people to return to Him, and who never forgets those who respond.

Are we living in another such time of waiting? If so, then the fires of our faith also may be rekindled as we meditate on Malachi and his message.

---

1. The Bible text used in this book is from the Revised Standard Version of the Bible, copyrighted 1946, 1952, © 1971, 1973. Used by permission.

2. From *The New English Bible*. Copyright © The Delegates of the Oxford University Press and the Syndics of the Cambridge University Press, 1961, 1970. Reprinted by permission.
3. *The Prophets of the Restoration* (New York: Robert Carter and Brothers, 1856), p. 337.
4. Joyce G. Baldwin, "Haggai, Zechariah, Malachi," *Tyndale Old Testament Commentaries* (London: The Tyndale Press, 1972), p. 211.
5. D. R. Jones, "Haggai, Zechariah and Malachi," *Torch Bible Commentary*, ed. John Marsh and Alan Richardson (London: SCM Press Ltd., 1962), p. 182.
6. H. B. Tristram, *The Natural History of the Bible* (New York: Pott, Young & Co., 1867), p. 111.
7. HOLY BIBLE *New International Version*, copyright © 1978, New York Bible Society. Used by permission.
8. *Aspects of the Old Testament* (London: Longmans, Green and Company, 1897), p. 203.

# Personal Learning Activities

1. Malachi's method as a prophet was that of (choose the correct answer from the list):
   (1) ___Sermon (3) ___Dialogue
   (2) ___Pantomime (4) ___Acted parables
2. The name *Malachi* means ____________
3. Malachi ministered during a time when his people were disillusioned, discouraged, and struggling. ___True ___False
4. The biblical concept of election is that God chose Israel based on (select the proper response from the list):
   (1) ___Israel's moral goodness (3) ___Israel's strength
   (2) ___God's love (4) ___Israel's size
5. Malachi said that proof of God's love for Israel was the devastation of ____________.
6. Malachi's favorite designation for God was ____________. (Choose the correct response from the list.)
   (1) ___Jehovah (3) ___God Most High
   (2) ___Lord of Hosts (4) ___The God of Abraham

Answers: 1. (3); 2. "My Messenger"; 3. True; 4. (2); 5. Edom; 6. (2).

# 2 How Have We Despised Your Name?

## Malachi 1:6 to 2:9

At the time of the Exiles' return in 538 BC, the land of Judah seems to have been governed by a council of elders, presided over by Zerubbabel and Joshua. (See Ezra 2:1-2,68-69; 3:1-2; 4:3.) Joshua probably served a long term as high priest. When he died, he was succeeded by his son Joiakim, who continued in office until Nehemiah's time.

The high priest's functions were expanded greatly in the postexilic period. The people increasingly came to rely on him rather than on the governor to represent them in their relations with the Persian authorities, especially since most of the governors seem to have been foreigners. Thus, the high priest assumed a leading role in the community's political life as well as its religious life. Perhaps this was one of the factors that influenced Malachi to give so much prominence to the priesthood in his preaching.

Malachi mounted a relentless attack on the priests, not because he was opposed to the priesthood, but because he believed in it so deeply. His view of the dignity of the priest's office is unsurpassed in the rest of the Old Testament. To him, the priests' irresponsible behavior was inexcusable precisely because so much was expected of them and so much depended on them. When they were faithful, the entire nation was blessed. But when they failed, the entire nation suffered the consequences.

The theme of Malachi 1:6 to 2:9 is the priests' failure to live up to their responsibility. Two basic charges were leveled against them: (1) They had shown contempt and disrespect for the Lord, the great King, through their disregard for the sacrificial system's requirements (1:6-14). (2) They had failed to fulfill their mission to teach the law of the Lord to the people (2:1-9).

# An Irresponsible Priesthood (1:6-14)

Often, one is helped in studying a Scripture passage to pick out key words and to examine how the author used them. The word "name" (v. 6) and the terms to "despise" (v. 6) and to "profane" (v. 12) seem to be the key words in 1:6-14.

First, let us examine the references to the divine name. Malachi 1:6-14 contains six references. Twice, God said that His name is "great" (v. 11), although the recognition of His greatness seemed to be limited to the nations outside Israel! This is one of the passage's major thrusts and one to which we will return. Note also that the Lord's name was honored through pure offerings of incense (v. 11), and that it was feared or reverenced (v. 14). But these acts of reverence took place "among the nations" (v. 14) and not in Israel. Finally, note that certain titles in this passage stressed the significance of God's name. He was called "father" and "master" (v. 6), and "King" (v. 14). The inescapable conclusion is that Malachi held God's name to be worthy of people's highest praise, reverence, and honor.

In Hebrew thought, a name was far more than just a convenient way to address another person. A person's name represented the essence of his or her being. This explains why the Bible gives so much attention to naming newborn infants. Furthermore, the revelation of God's name to a person was viewed as a sign of special favor. Jacob was willing to wrestle all night to try to receive such a favor. (See Gen. 32:29-30.) Moses was reluctant to undertake the task of leading the Israelites out of Egypt unless God would reveal to him His name. (See Ex. 3:13-15.) To know God's name was to know God, His holiness, His power, and His love. To honor His name was to honor God. To despise His name was the height of blasphemy and sacrilege.

Perhaps the Hebrew concept of God's name will help us to understand better why Jesus taught His followers to pray:

> "Our Father who art in heaven,
> *Hallowed be thy name*" (Matt. 6:9).

The responsibility rests just as heavily on us as it did on Malachi's listeners to reverence and honor God's name. Furthermore, we never should forget that God has exalted Christ highly and has bestowed on Him a name that is above every name, and that at Jesus' name every knee should bow and every tongue confess that He is Lord. (See Phil. 2:9-11.)

Among the nations, God's name was exalted (Mal. 1:11) and feared (v. 14); but the same could not be said of Israel. The Jews' priests, who should have set the example for the entire nation, were guilty of despising (v. 6) and profaning (v. 12) His great name. Of course, they never would have said, *May the Lord's name be despised and profaned!* But they were guilty of despising and profaning God's name through their slovenly attitude toward the Temple and its services. They were treating the Temple with contempt and were offering culls and runts as sacrifices instead of their best animals. In Malachi's words, they were despising the Lord's table (the altar, v. 7) and the food (the sacrifices, v. 12) offered on it. The modern equivalent to this would be a minister who secretly chafed under his responsibility and regarded the church's services as a waste of time. To render true worship to God is to honor His name; to be careless and irreverent in worship is to despise his name.

**Prodigal Sons and Unfaithful Servants (v. 6)**

Father, Master, and King are the titles that Malachi used to describe God (vv. 6,14). The only appropriate response to such a great God would be honor, respect, and reverence. The priests of the fifth century BC were showing the opposite response—dishonor, disrespect, and irreverence.

Malachi set a trap for the unsuspecting priests by first stating a proposition that they would accept readily. They fully subscribed to the rule, "'A son honors his father, and a servant his master.'" Their society was based on proper respect for persons in positions of authority. A state of anarchy would have resulted if the sons had ceased to honor their fathers or the servants had ceased to fear their masters. Their law was clear and plain about such matters.

Once the priests had assented to Malachi's opening statement, he proceeded to draw an obvious but deeply disturbing analogy. Since the priests professed to believe that God was their Father and Master, why did they not show Him the honor and fear that was due Him? God had expected from them a reverence that found pleasure in His service and a love that dreaded to offend Him, but they had closed their ears to His demands. Now, they found themselves trapped by the prophet's accusation. They could give no answer to justify their behavior. They were guilty of having acted like prodigal sons and like wicked servants.

Malachi left no doubt that the primary responsibility for Israel's deplorable situation rested on the priests. He called them *despisers of my* (God's) *name* (literal translation). This meant that their attitude toward God was one of scorn and contempt. The prophet's word to describe the priests' action means *to raise the head disdainfully*. In essence, they had thumbed their noses at God.

Stung by the prophet's accusation against them, the priests issued a strong disclaimer: "'How have we despised thy name?'" Their question was rhetorical, which meant that they expected the Lord to say, *I'm sorry! I must have made a mistake!* Their question shows that they were tragically sincere in the belief that they were being accused falsely. They had fallen into the last stages of self-deception where conscience ceased to work as an accusing witness; they even had fallen into a hypocrisy that did not know itself to be hypocritical. When persons deliberately and repeatedly choose to do wrong, the time may come when they are incapable of discerning between right and wrong and are unwilling to accept responsibility for wrongdoing. Perhaps such a condition could be described best as atrophy of the will.

**Further Accusations and Denials (vv. 7-9)**

The prophet answered the priests' protests of innocence by enlarging on the accusations he previously had made against them. He told them that they were despising the Lord by offering desecrated food at His table (v. 7). This is metaphorical language, for "food" refers to the gifts of grain and flesh brought to the Lord, while "table" refers to the altar on which the gifts were given. Perhaps one could understand the priests' outrageous action better by comparing it to someone today who would invite an honored guest to his or her home and then serve the guest a plate of rotten food. That the guest would interpret this as a deliberate insult goes without saying. How much more is the Lord insulted by those whose worship is little more than a mockery?

Old Testament regulations demanded that animals which people offered as sacrifices should be without blemish. (See Lev. 22:17-25.) Though the priests whom Malachi confronted were familiar with these regulations, they were offering animals that were blind, mutilated, and diseased (Mal. 1:8*a*). Robert C. Dentan has labeled such behavior "an outward and visible sign of an inward and spiritual *dis*-grace, since a man who will deliberately offer the worst animal in his flock on God's altar is obviously not right with God in his heart."[1]

An idiomatic expression occurs twice in verse 8, and in both instances it is translated as a question: "Is that no evil?" However, the Hebrew text gives no indication that this expression was intended as a question. The same type of idiom occurs in Proverbs 28:24, where it is rendered: "He who robs his father or his mother and says, 'That is no transgression,' is the companion of a man who destroys." In the light of this usage, the following is offered as a paraphrase of verse 8*a*: When you offer blind animals in sacrifice, you say, 'There's nothing wrong with it!' and when you offer animals that are lame or diseased, you say, 'There's nothing wrong with it!' The priests pretended that the weak and sickly animals they brought to the altar were in prime condition. They were neither the first nor the last to exaggerate the value of their gifts to the Lord.

The prophet challenged the priests to offer to their governor such paltry gifts as they had been offering to God (Mal. 1:8*b*). The irony of his suggestion should not be overlooked. He was saying that they had greater respect for their governor than they had for God. Malachi knew that if they began to treat their governor as they had been treating God, they soon would be in serious trouble. Today, are God's people perhaps more conscientious about their obligations to the government than they are about their obligations to God? If so, what does this indicate about their priorities?

Sometimes, Malachi has been accused of giving too much attention to such sins as offering inferior animals and withholding tithes. (See 3:8-10.) However, in his defense, he was no mere advocate of tradition. He never supported the performance of ritual for ritual's sake. For him, an act of worship was not an end in itself; it was the outward expression of one's inner attitude

"'When you offer . . . animals . . . that are lame and sick, is that no evil?'" (Mal. 1:8).

toward God. This was why Malachi insisted that only the best was good enough for God. Furthermore, he taught that worship that pleased the Lord could be offered only by those whose hearts had been cleansed and purified. (See 3:3-4.) He also attacked the social ills of his day and called for a radical turning to the Lord. (See 3:5-7.) Thus, to say that Malachi was concerned only with the externals of religion would be unfair.

Verse 9 is an exhortation to the priests to intercede before God on Israel's behalf. To **entreat the favor of God** literally means *to make pleasant the face of God*. It was a bold expression implying that through intercessary prayer the marks of anger and displeasure could be removed from God's face. By Malachi's time, it had come to be used as a common metaphor for prayer. The prophet's exhortation was meant to be taken seriously.

To determine the exact relationship between the two halves of verse 9 is difficult. In the Hebrew text, the second half of the verse begins, "from your hand this has been"; but to what "this" refers is not clear. I prefer to interpret it as a reference to the deplorable situation that existed in Israel at the time the prophet spoke. By laying the blame for the situation at the priests' feet, Malachi reinforced his call to them to engage in intercessory prayer for the afflicted nation. Perhaps he thought that by so doing, they could be equipped again for the ministry they almost had forfeited.

**When Temples Become Liabilities (vv. 10-11)**

The true gravity of Israel's situation became evident when God called for a volunteer to close the Temple doors and to put out the altar fires so that the whole sorry business could be halted (v. 10*a*). Whether this reference was to the gates that led into the larger Temple area, the gates of the outer court, or the doors of the inner court is not clear. The last seems most likely. Closing the doors to the inner court would have barred the priests from the altar of burnt offerings without having to seal off the entire Temple area. Seemingly, the Lord had come to regard the sacrifices in the Temple as more of a liability than an asset.

The latter part of verse 10 states the Lord's rejection of any further sacrifices that the officiating priests offered. They had been laboring under the delusion that their sacrifices were indispensable to the Lord. They thought that poor sacrifices given grudgingly were better than no sacrifices at all. The prophet informed them that the Lord had no need of their despicable gifts. At first, the word for "offering" (Mal. 1:10*b*) referred to grain offerings; but by Malachi's time, it had come to mean any and all types of offerings. Thus, verse 10 is as strong a repudiation of empty ritual as a Hebrew prophet ever voiced.

From a theological point of view, perhaps the most interesting statement in Malachi is in verse 11. In contrast to the shoddy worship being offered in Jerusalem, it indicates a high and noble worship being offered to the Lord throughout the world. The global extent of such worship is indicated by "from the rising of the sun to its setting," "among the nations," and "in every place." The adjective used to describe such worship is "pure." Furthermore, reference is made twice to the recognition of the greatness of the Lord's name "among the nations." One hardly can escape the conclusion that the contrast between the situation in Jerusalem and throughout the rest of the world was drawn deliberately.

*"'In every place incense is offered to my name, and a pure offering'" (Mal. 1:11).*

How is one to identify those who "from the rising of the sun to its setting" were offering acceptable worship to the Lord? Across the centuries, three approaches have claimed support. The first may be termed the eschatological approach. It arose first among early Christian expositors who understood the verse as a prophecy of the rejection of the Jews and the adoption of the Gentiles. The acceptable sacrifices were identified with Christ's sacrifice, or with the commemoration of that sacrifice in the Lord's Supper, or in a purely spiritual sense with the prayers and praises of God's people.

The second view may be called the dispersion view. According to this view, Malachi was commending the worship being offered to God by Jews living outside Palestine. Supposedly, the Jews of the dispersion were more mindful of the Lord and of the requirements of worship than their lax compatriots in Jerusalem. The only place known to have served as a place of worship for Jews living outside Palestine during Malachi's lifetime was at Elephantine on the southern end of a small island in the Nile River in Egypt.

The third approach is the literal approach. Most scholars believe that Malachi's words should be given their most natural and obvious meaning. Note that Malachi lived at a time when the sacrifices that were offered in Jersualem were an insult to God, betraying the worshipers' attitude that anything was good enough for God. Malachi argued that their dishonest worship did not stack up against the honest worship that was offered among the nations. Perhaps as thoughtful pagans began to repudiate the more sensual and polytheistic elements of their religions, Jews could accept them as proselytes. Of course, this does not mean that such proselytes did not need to be taught a purer faith, or that sincerity of spirit was the sole factor in true religion. If this approach is correct, 1:11 certainly is the most generous estimate of Gentile religion to be found in the Old Testament.

Verse 12 restates the charge against the priests, as if the prophet wanted to seal the indictment against them. Their insolent behavior rendered their sacrifices unacceptable.

**Burned-Out Priests (vv. 13-14)**

"Burn-out" seemed to have been a problem for ministers and priests long before the twentieth century. According to the opening line of verse 13, the priests in Malachi's day were saying: "'What a weariness this is'" (RSV), or "'How irksome!'" (NEB).[2] Opinions differ widely about how these words should be interpreted. The Septuagint reads: "These services are troublesome." This implies that the priests were making excuse for the poor quality of their sacrifices by claiming that these were given out of their poverty and that they could afford nothing better.

Kimchi, a medieval Jewish commentator, suggested another interpretation.[3] His paraphrase read: "'What a heavy burden this lamb is!'" Supposedly, the priests spoke these words as they approached the altar in a spirit of feigned weariness. They pretended to puff and pant under the sacrificial lamb's weight, although it was so skinny that a strong gust of wind would have blown it away!

The most widely accepted interpretation represents the priests as saying: *How irksome is the service of God!* According to this view, they had lost the sense of their calling's sacredness and had come to regard the duties of their office as tedious drudgery. E. B. Pusey's comments regarding such a spirit of boredom apply to all persons who aspire to serve God in whatever age: "The service of God is its own reward. If not, it becomes a greater toil, with less reward from this earth, than the things of this earth. Our only choice is between love and weariness."[4]

Verses 13*b*-14 picture the priests treating God with contempt and scorn. Through Malachi, God said: "You sniff at me" (v. 13*b*). They offered Him their poorest animals. They even substituted sickly animals for the healthy animals they had vowed to give Him (v. 14). Such behavior was all the more reprehensible because of who He is, "a great King"!

Substituting a sickly animal for a healthy one that had been promised to the Lord in fulfillment of a vow was all the more reprehensible because a worshiper did not have to give votive offerings. They were offerings freely given to fulfill vows that had been made voluntarily in times of personal need. The law required that only male animals without blemish should be used in such offerings. The ancient Talmud contains an interesting bit of advice about making and keeping vows: "'Promise little, and do much.'" Abraham only promised a morsel of bread but fetched a calf tender and good (*Priqe Aboth* 1:15; see Gen. 18:1-8). In other words, always do more than you promise, not less.

## Leaders Who Mislead (2:1-9)

In 2:1-9, Malachi continued his attack on the unfaithful priests. Earlier, he had charged them with desecrating the Temple worship. Now, he accused them of having failed in their teaching duties; thus, they had misled the people.

In Old Testament times, the teaching ministry was assigned to the Temple priests. This is stated clearly in verse 7: "For the lips of a priest should guard knowledge, and men should seek instruction from his mouth, for he is the messenger of the Lord of hosts." Malachi, whose name meant "my messenger," was placing a priest's call and commission on the same level with his. In several instances recorded in the Old Testament, the people were told to seek instruction from the mouth of a priest.

To be charged with the responsibility of teaching and directing God's people is a task that is not to be taken lightly. James commented on the weight of this responsibility in the context of the church: "Let not many of you become teachers, my brethren, for you know that we who teach shall be judged with greater strictness" (Jas. 3:1).

Malachi addressed priests who had neglected their duty to instruct the people; thus, they had corrupted the Levitical covenant that gave them the right to be priests. For this reason, the priests were threatened with expulsion from their sacred office and with public humiliation. No prophet ever spoke harsher words against the priests. Perhaps this was because no other prophet ever had a higher ideal for the priesthood than Malachi.

### Appropriate Punishment for Faithless Priests (vv. 1-3)

Malachi confronted the priests with a decree of destruction that is called "command" (v. 1). Before pronouncing judgment on them, he appealed to them to listen, to take God's words to heart, and to give glory to God's name (v. 2).

*"'And now, O priests, this command is for you'"*
*(Mal. 2:1).*

The Hebrew word translated **listen** also meant *to obey*. The Jews did not think that one truly had heard unless and until hearing led to obedience. In the Old Testament, the "heart" (v. 2) was the seat of the intellect and the will rather than of the emotions. "To give glory to . . . [God's] name" was an appropriate summary of the priesthood's whole duty. **Glory** had the underlying meaning of *heaviness* or *weightiness*. A man's glory consisted of his honor, his splendor, his reputation, and his wealth. God's glory included all that could be apprehended of His presence on earth—that is, His character and essential being as revealed through His people and through His mighty acts in their history. Therefore, when Malachi exhorted the priests to give glory to the Lord's name, he meant that through their righteous living they should mirror God's true image to other persons. One could have no higher goal in life than this. This is what living for God's glory means.

Malachi pronounced an ominous threat against the priests. If they persisted in their sin, the Lord would send "the curse" on them (v. 2). The Hebrew has the definite article; it is "*the* curse." In Semitic thought, the blessing and the curse were eminently real and concrete; they were not just the expression of a good or bad wish about someone. (See Deut. 30:19-20.) The Israelites called their life-giving, protective force the "blessing," while its evil counterpart—all that weakened or destroyed life—was called the "curse." The curse was a potent weapon in God's arsenal, for when it was unleashed it sped like a well-aimed missile against evildoers. Johs. Pederson has described the lot of those upon whom the curse fell as one of hopeless misery and failure: "Close to sin lies the *curse*, their mutual relation being as righteousness to blessing. The sinner is charged with the curse, for the curse is the dissolution which takes place in the soul of the sinner. It is as a poisonous, consuming substance that destroys and undermines, so that the soul falls to pieces and its strength is exhausted. . . . The cursed is the man for whom everything fails."[5]

Even the priestly blessings would be turned into curses (v. 2). Whether the blessings were those that the priests pronounced on the people or the blessings that the priests should have received by virtue of their office is debated. Probably, all of the privileges that the priests enjoyed were to be recalled. Every good that they previously had enjoyed would be replaced by that dreaded evil, the curse.

As if to mount threat on threat, the Lord announced that He also would cut off the priests' offspring (v. 3*a*). The hereditary office of the priesthood would come to an end because no Levitical priests would be left to carry it on.

The Lord saved His worst threat against the proud priests until last. He announced that He would smear the dung of the priests' sacrifices on their faces (v. 3*b*). The dung was that which accumulated in the Temple area during the sacrificial offerings. According to the law, it was unclean and had to be removed to a place outside the camp and burned. If a priest came in contact with the dung, he was considered to be unclean. (See Num. 19:5-7.) The final phrase in Malachi 2:3 perhaps could be translated best: "And one shall take you away with it" (KJV). The meaning seems to be that those who came to remove the dung from the Temple area would remove the dung-covered priests along with it. This was Malachi's interpretation of the cleansing of the Temple! What a terrible way to treat a proud priesthood!

**God's Covenant with the Priests (vv. 4-7)**

God's purpose in judging the priests was that His covenant with their ancestor Levi might be reinforced: "that my covenant with Levi may hold" (v. 4). Judgment was meant to be redemptive and not merely punitive. (See 3:3-4.)

The covenant with Levi usually is taken to mean the one that God made with Phinehas recorded in Numbers 25:10-13: "And the Lord said to Moses, 'Phinehas the son of Eleazar, son of Aaron the priest, has turned back my wrath from the people of Israel, in that he was jealous with my jealousy among them, so that I did not consume the people of Israel in my jealousy. Therefore say, "Behold, I give to him my covenant of peace; and it shall be to him, and to his descendants after him, the covenant of a perpetual priesthood, because he was jealous for his God, and made atonement for the people of Israel."'" The covenant with Phinehas, a descendant of Levi, was the charter under which the tribe of Levi remained in possession of the priesthood across the centuries.

Malachi 2:5-7 contains what many interpreters regard as the

highest view of the priestly office in the Old Testament. These verses picture the Lord as if He were reminiscing about the days of old, the time when His covenant with the sons of Levi was honored and respected. It was a covenant based on mutual obligations. On His part, God had promised the sons of Levi life and peace; and He had kept His promise (v. 5*a*). On their part, they had promised to fear Him; and this they had done, giving reverence to His name (v. 5*b*). It had been a perfect covenant that had been kept perfectly.

In the Old Testament period, the priests were regarded as the official custodians and administrators of the law; and they were charged with instructing the people. Malachi pointed back to a time when faithful priests imparted sound teaching and when they spoke no word of injustice (v. 6*a*).

Sound teaching was reinforced by exemplary living. The faithful priest walked with God "in peace and uprightness" (v. 6*b*). Elsewhere in the Old Testament, only Enoch (Gen. 5:22,24) and Noah (Gen. 6:9) were said to have "walked with God," although Micah listed walking humbly with God as required of all God's people (Mic. 6:8). To walk "with God" denoted a more intimate fellowship than walking "after" Him.

The concluding line in verse 6 describes the influence that the priests of old exerted on others' lives. Because they were men of piety and integrity, instructed the people with sound teaching, and walked close to God, they caused many to turn back from iniquity. This is one of the highest commendations that could be given to a minister of God.

Jonathan Edwards preached for twenty-three years, from 1727 to 1750, at a church in Northampton, Massachusetts. Inside the church that he served hangs a bronze plaque commemorating his years of service. The tribute paid to him concludes with the full text of Malachi 2:6. How many ministers have you known to whom these words would apply?

Verse 7 concludes Malachi's description of the ideal priest. This ideal was realized when the priest's lips became a storehouse of knowledge and when the people could seek instruction from his mouth. The priest was called "the messenger of the Lord of hosts," a title found nowhere else in the Old Testament with reference to priests (with the possible exception of Eccl. 5:6). This certainly is one of the finest verses in Malachi.

Its recognition of the priest's importance as a teacher is unsurpassed in the rest of the Old Testament. It should be compared with 2 Chronicles 15:3, where the greatest tragedy that could befall Israel is described as being left "without the true God, and without a teaching priest and without law." What do you think this indicates about the importance of teaching in the church's total life? On whom does this responsibility rest today?

**God's Judgment on Faithless Leaders (vv. 8-9)**

The priests' failure in Malachi's day was in sharp contrast to the fidelity of former priests. The contrast is made sharper by the emphatic way verse 8 begins: "But *you!*"

The first charge laid at the priests' feet was that they had turned aside from the way (v. 8*a*). Earlier priests had walked with God, but these had departed from God's way and were pursuing their own selfish goals. The second charge grew out of the first: The wayward priests had caused many persons to stumble through the priests' example and teaching (v. 8*b*). Only eternity can reveal the perverse influence of God's ministers who betray their high calling. The third charge was that the priests had violated the covenant of Levi (v. 8*c*). This meant that they no longer could function as the Lord's priests. This was the most serious charge, for no wrong was so great as that of breaking a covenant with the Lord.

This section ends with a description of the fate in store for the rejected priests. The Lord announced that He would make them despised and abased before all of the people because of their contemptible behavior (v. 9). Their guilt was summed up in the accusation that they had not kept God's ways and that they had shown partiality in their instruction.

The last accusation suggests that in their teaching and preaching, they had allowed themselves to be unduly influenced by the rich and the powerful, a vice not unknown among ministers in our day. Whenever a minister trims his message in order not to offend powerful elements in his congregation, he is inviting the Lord's reprimand and the world's contempt.

# Lessons for Life from Malachi 1:6 to 2:9

*The Lord has high expectations for persons who would serve as His ministers.*—The reason is that they have the potential either for great good or for great harm. No more lasting influence for good can be exerted than the life of a faithful and dedicated servant of the Lord. On the other hand, no greater harm to Christ's cause can be done than that resulting from one of His servants' moral and spiritual failure. The call to ministry is a high calling; it never should be undertaken lightly. Anyone who answers such a call should be prepared to do whatever is necessary to meet its demands.

*Those who answer God's call to ministry must have a consuming love for ministry, or else they will suffer from endless boredom and fatigue.*—The modern term to describe such boredom and fatigue is "ministerial burn-out." For ministers to lose the sense of their calling's sacredness and to chafe under its demands is easy. A certain amount of boredom and fatigue is inevitable in any vocation, but when these become unmanageable in a minister's life, he should examine his priorities and perhaps seek a trusted friend's counsel.

Truly effective ministers always have found serving God to be its own reward. They neither have been turned on by praise nor have been turned off by criticism. They have not heaped up self-pity by comparing their salaries unfavorably with those of other professionals. They have not regarded the call to ministry as a sacrifice or as an ordeal to be endured but as a grand and glorious privilege that they would not have missed for all the world.

A missionary was offered a position with a large firm that was doing business in the country where he was serving. The position carried a salary that was much higher than what the missionary had been receiving. When he declined the offer, the firm's officials returned with an even higher salary offer. Again, he declined. The officials, reacting in amazement, asked: "How much salary would persuade you to join our firm?" The missionary responded: "Oh, it's not a question of your salary not being big enough. It's just that your job isn't big enough!"

*The outward acts of worship that we perform are a reliable gauge of the quality and vitality of our commitment to God.*—For us to give God the leftovers in our lives—leftover time, money, interest, and strength—is not enough. We would not dare even to treat our government in this fashion.

The priests of Malachi's day acted as though they thought that anything was good enough for God. Contrast their attitude with that of countless Christians today who are indicating that only the best is good enough for God. Included are custodians who give loving care to God's house; choir members who spend long hours training to sing His praises; Sunday School teachers who study diligently to teach their classes; visitors who call on the sick, the lonely, and the lost; and faithful Christians everywhere who honor God with their gifts of time and money. Jesus had such as these in mind when He said: "'You are the salt of the earth; . . . . You are the light of the world'" (Matt. 5:13*a*,14*a*).

---

1. "The Book of Malachi," *The Interpreter's Bible* (Nashville: Abingdon Press, 1956), 6:1119.
2. From *The New English Bible*. Copyright © The Delegates of the Oxford University Press and the Syndics of the Cambridge University Press, 1961, 1970. Reprinted by permission.
3. See Eli Cashdan, *The Twelve Prophets*, The Soncino Books of the Bible (London: The Soncino Press, 1959), p. 341.
4. *The Minor Prophets*, (New York: Funk and Wagnalls, 1885), 2:474.
5. *Israel*, (London: Oxford University Press, 1973), 1:437,440.

# Personal Learning Activities

1. To the Hebrews, what did a person's name represent?
2. Malachi left no doubt that the primary responsibility for Israel's deplorable situation rested with the ____________.
3. To stress vividly the failure to honor God, Malachi used ____________ and ____________ as a proposition that was known to be true. (Choose the correct

answers from the list.)

(1) A son's honoring his father

(2) A subject's honoring a king

(3) A wife's honoring her husband

(4) A servant's honoring his master

4. The prophet indicted his hearers for despising God's name by using it in profanity. ___True ___False
5. The priests had come to see their calling and duties as a challenge and a delight. ___True ___False
6. In what additional duty had the priests failed?
7. The most serious charge against the priests was that they ________________________________.

Answers: 1. The person's essence or being; 2. Priests; 3. (1),(4); 4. False; 5. False; 6. In teaching the people; 7. Broke God's covenant with them.

# 3 Why Are We Faithless to One Another?

When the first divisions of the Book of Malachi were examined, the note was made that they dealt mainly with the priests' sins. In the previous study, the nature of their wrongdoing was considered. They had profaned the Temple by presenting unworthy offerings at the altar; they had despised the priestly covenant through ungodly living; and they had caused many persons to stumble through the shameful example they set.

"Like people, like priest" was an adage at least as old as Hosea's time. (See Hos. 4:9.) Hosea used it to describe the judgment that would fall with equal severity on people and priests in the eighth century BC.

The saying also may be interpreted to mean that a nation's character largely is determined by its spiritual leaders' characters. When the leaders are lax in their moral standards, greedy for success and recognition, self-serving, and irreverent toward God, to expect that the people will be different is unrealistic. Inevitably, people pattern their lives after the example that their leaders set.

Malachi was distressed that a corrupted priesthood had produced a corrupted society. To him, the most obvious proof of this was the fact that the Jewish men were divorcing their Jewish wives and were taking younger wives from the pagan nations that surrounded them. The prophet saw this as a violation of the covenant of brotherhood that had bound Israelites to one another from the beginning (v. 10). He also saw the practice of divorce as an act of treachery against God—profaning the sacred unity of Israel, the people whom God had intended to be His sanctuary or dwelling place on earth (vv. 11-12). Finally, he saw divorce as a violation of the marriage covenant—a covenant that God had witnessed—and a repudiation of the divorced Jewish wives' rights (vv. 13-14).

The result of the practice of divorce was that Jewish worship was ineffective. The Lord no longer accepted the people's offerings, although they wept, groaned, and covered the altar with tears (v. 13).

God never condones people's mean-spirited and underhanded ways, no matter how high they pile His altar with their sacrifices. When they meet Him in judgment, the face He turns toward them will be a reflection of the face they have turned toward others. His countenance in eternity will mirror their countenance in time. If they have been crooked and perverse toward others, He will reveal Himself to them in judgment. But if they have been loyal, blameless, and pure toward others, He will show Himself to them as loyal, blameless, and pure. Judgment does not determine a person's character; it merely confirms it.

## Behavior That Weakens Corporate Witness (2:10-12)

Sometimes, a person says: "What I am and the way I live is nobody's business but my own!" Of course, the statement has a certain amount of truth, for in the final analysis each person is accountable for the way he or she lives. But if this statement means that people's actions affect no one but themselves, then the speakers are sadly mistaken. Above all others, Christians need to remember that their actions either strengthen the church's corporate witness or weaken it. How tragic to see a church whose witness is being negated by some members' unwholesome behavior!

Malachi confronted a somewhat similar situation in ancient Israel. By dealing faithlessly with one another, the Jews were destroying the bonds of union that held them together (v. 10) and were violating God's purpose that their nation should become His sanctuary or dwelling place on earth (v. 11). The passage 2:10-12 ends with a prayer that the one guilty of such acts of sin should be punished appropriately (v. 12).

**Destroying the Bonds of Brotherhood (v. 10)**

God's purpose for the Jews—who shared a common ancestry, a common heritage, and a common faith—was that they should live together in the bonds of brotherhood. Perhaps, that ideal is expressed best in Psalm 133:1-3:

> Behold, how good and
> pleasant it is
> when brothers dwell in unity!
> It is like the precious oil upon the
> head,
> running down upon the beard,
> upon the beard of Aaron,
> running down on the collar of
> his robes!
> It is like the dew of Hermon,
> which falls on the mountains of
> Zion!
> For there the Lord has commanded
> the blessing,
> life for evermore.

"Blessing" and "life for evermore" are contingent on believers dwelling together in unity. The opposite of this is for persons in the faith to live together like proverbial "cats and dogs." No sorrier spectacle presents itself than that of a church or a denomination whose witness is discredited because of internal strife and divisions. The Bible states clearly the Lord's response to such a situation:

> There are six things which the
> Lord hates,
> seven which are an abomination
> to him:
> haughty eyes, a lying tongue,
> and hands that shed innocent
> blood,

a heart that devises wicked plans,
feet that make haste to run to
evil,
a false witness who breathes out lies,
and a man who sows discord
among brothers (Prov. 6:16-19).

Malachi 2:10 begins with two questions, both of which demand an affirmative response. "Have we not all one father?" Answer: Yes! "Has not one God created us?" Answer: Yes!

Some have interpreted "one father" and "one God" to be parallel terms, both referring to God. However, neither the Revised Standard Version nor the *New English Bible* capitalizes the word "father," thus suggesting that it does not refer to God but to an earthly father. The most commonly accepted interpretation is that it refers either to Adam or to one of the patriarchs—in this case either Abraham or Jacob. If one were to choose one of the three, then Abraham probably would be the best choice. He was regarded universally as the father of the Hebrew people. On the other hand, Malachi paid special attention to Jacob throughout his book. This suggests that Jacob may have been the one whom he regarded as the father of the nation. (See 1:2; 2:12; 3:6.)

Verse 10 sometimes has been cited as a proof-text for the universal brotherhood of all mankind. However, this is not the point of this text. On the contrary, as the context shows, Malachi was addressing fellow Jews and reminding them of their essential unity and of their distinct identity as God's people. That Jews, bound together by race ("one father") and by religion ("one God"), should act treacherously against one another so as to profane their forefathers' covenant distressed Malachi (v. 10*b*). Like Esau of old, they had despised their birthright. (See Gen. 25:29-34.)

**Profaning the Lord's Sanctuary (vv. 11-12)**

In this passage, God's people are identified by four overlapping terms: Judah (v. 11), Israel (v. 11), Jerusalem (v. 11), and Jacob (v. 12). The prophet's charge was that the entire nation was ripe for judgment because the people had been faithless, had committed abomination, and had profaned the Lord's sanctuary by marrying the daughter of a foreign god.

**To be faithless** literally means *to deal treacherously.* (See the same charge in v. 10.) The broader meaning is *to betray a trust, to be unfaithful to a commitment, or to undermine another's position.* An "abomination" is a custom or an action that is grossly out of harmony with the Lord's revealed will and character. It describes the practices of God's people that are most abhorrent to the Lord.

Judah had profaned the Lord's sanctuary (v. 11*b*). Both here and in verse 10, the word translated **to profane** means *to destroy the value of something by defacing it or piercing it with a sharp instrument.*

"The sanctuary of the Lord" could refer to the Temple or to the community of Israel. The latter sometimes was designated as the Lord's sanctuary or dwelling place on earth. (See Ps. 114:1-2.) Malachi probably meant Israel, since in verse 10 he had described the Jews' unity as being threatened by the faithless behavior of brother against brother.

By a slight modification of the punctuation in the latter part of verse 11, a possible translation is: *for Judah has profaned the sanctuary of the Lord, in that he loved and married the daughter of a foreign god.* "The daughter of a foreign god" can mean that the people of Judah were worshiping a foreign goddess, since "daughter" is singular. (See Jer. 44:15-19.) This interpretation has the support of the Greek Version, which reads: "and has gone after other gods."

In spite of these considerations, most scholars interpret verse 11*b* as a condemnation of intermarriage with idolatrous women from the surrounding nations. Thus, The *New English Bible* renders: "Judah has violated the holiness of the Lord by loving and marrying daughters of a foreign god."[1] Support for this interpretation is found in the fact that intermarriage of Jewish men with non-Jewish women was one of the most urgent problems that Ezra and Nehemiah had to face. (See Ezra 9:1 to 10:44; Neh. 13:23-27.)

Deuteronomy has regulations covering mixed marriages: (1) Deuteronomy 7:3 forbade all intermarriage with the seven groups that occupied Canaan. (2) Deuteronomy 23:3-4 imposed a ban on persons of Ammonite and Moabite descent. (3) Deuteronomy 23:7-8 excluded a person of Edomite or Egyptian

*"'Judah has . . . married the daughter of a foreign god'"* (Mal. 2:11).

descent from the congregation of the Lord until the third generation. (4) On the other hand, Deuteronomy 21:10-13 expressly allowed an Israelite to marry a foreign captive woman. Violations of these regulations may have been fairly common, for Ruth the Moabitess married Boaz the Israelite and became King David's ancestress. (See Ruth 4:13-17.)

When Malachi condemned marriage with "the daughter of a foreign god," he meant with a woman who actually was an idolatress. Therefore, he deliberately chose an expression that did not rule out the possibility of marriage with foreign-born women if they were converts to Israel's faith. The Old Testament consistently opposed marriages where the possibility existed that idolatry would be introduced into Israel. (See Ex. 34:11-16; Deut. 7:1-6.) Such marriages were a threat to the nation's existence as God's covenant people.

Verse 12 is in the form of a covenant curse. The prophet called on the Lord to cut off all offspring from the households of those who had profaned His holiness by marrying foreign women. This curse is similar to the one that had been pronounced against the disobedient priests. (See 2:2-3.)

**Any to witness or answer** has puzzled commentators. The literal meaning is: *one awakening and one answering (the waking one and the answering one).* Probably, this was an idiom that meant all members of a man's family, both present and future. This is how the Targum and Syriac versions understood it, for they rendered it: "May the Lord cut off . . . both son and grandson." The Vulgate reads: "both teacher and pupil," apparently on the assumption that the teacher *awakens* and the pupil *answers*. By a slight change in the text, the Revised Standard Version reads: "any to witness or answer." The meaning of this translation would be that all offenders in Israel would be deprived of legal protection and left without witness or defender in court.

The last part of the curse asked that those who married pagan women have no one left in their households to perform the duty of sacrifice. The same attitude toward sacrifice is reflected in 2:12 as in 1:10, namely, that sacrifice ceases to serve any useful purpose when it is performed by those who ignore God's moral demands. Both passages teach that God is not dependent on sacrifice and would prefer to see it abolished rather than to have it continued under the circumstances that Malachi confronted. The lesson that might be drawn from this is that inattention to God's moral demands makes worship a sham and a pretense. Proverbs 15:8 states:

> The sacrifice of the wicked is an
> abomination to the Lord,
> but the prayer of the upright
> is his delight.

## The Problem of Divorce (2:13-16)

In addition to taking wives from among idolatrous neighbors, the men of Judah were cruelly divorcing their Jewish wives. Malachi implied that they did this because their wives no longer were young and attractive. (See v. 14.) The men took younger, prettier wives from among their non-Jewish neighbors without raising questions of religion.

Almost every American family, of whatever size, has been touched in some way by the problem of divorce. The incidence of divorce in our society has reached epidemic proportions. Social analysts have tried to forecast the long-term effects of this problem on future generations; and some of their forecasts are disturbing, to say the least. This makes Malachi's message on this subject all the more relevant for today. He was the only prophet who dealt with the problem in any detail.

**Marital Problems and Personal Spirituality (vv. 13-14)**

Verse 13 adds a charge to the one contained in verses 10-12. Besides marrying pagan women, the men of Judah were divorcing their Jewish wives. One possible motive for their action was lust, the desire for younger and more sensual wives. A second possible motive was prestige. Since the non-Jewish nations held the reins of power, to have a non-Jewish wife would have been an economic and political advantage.

Since the Jewish men who married pagan women first had divorced their Jewish wives, the tears that covered the Lord's altar (v. 13) may have been those of the divorced wives. Re-

*"'You cover the Lord's altar with tears . . . because he no longer regards the offering'" (Mal. 2:13).*

jected and abandoned by their husbands, they may have gone to the Temple to complain of their cruel lot and to pour out their grief before the Lord. According to this interpretation, the Lord, who was moved to pity at the sight of their tears, announced that He no longer would accept the sacrifices of the men who were responsible for the divorced wives' suffering. No sadder plight existed in the ancient world than that of the castoff wife.

A second view regards the tears, the weeping, and the groaning as coming from the men of Judah who had been denounced for marrying foreign wives and divorcing their Jewish wives. They came to the altar, bringing sacrifices and asking the Lord's favor on them. But their sacrifices were rejected. How did they know this? Because their prayers were unanswered and the Lord's favor was not forthcoming.

Then, the men resorted to tears, groaning, and weeping. They had the mistaken notion that they could overcome God's reluctance to bless them if they wept loudly enough. They were willing to do anything to gain His favor—except repent. But God saw through their cloak of piety. He knew that their tears were "crocodile tears," for the real sufferers were the wives whom the men had repudiated. Therefore, God refused to regard or accept the men's offerings.

When the men of Judah learned that God had rejected their sacrifices, they pretended not to know the reason why. As if oblivious of any wrongdoing, they exclaimed: "'Why does he not?'" (v. 14). Their question opened the door for the prophet to deal with the problem of divorce.

Note that in verse 14, Malachi described the Lord as the silent witness to the marriage covenant. The Old Testament contains no reference to a religious ceremony accompanying marriages; but even without such a formality, God had been a witness to the marriage contracts. Those who dealt treacherously with a trusting spouse had to answer to Him.

Three terms in verse 14 describe the relationship between a man and his wife. The first, "wife of your youth," indicates that the prophet was referring to marriages contracted during the early years of youth. Even today, the custom in many parts of the world is for marriages to be arranged while the participants still are quite young.

The second term, "your companion," never is used again in

the Old Testament to refer to the husband-wife relationship. Elsewhere, it is applied to the relationship of a man to his male companions or friends (see Ps. 45:7; Eccl. 4:10; Dan. 2:17-18). To say that Malachi was championing the equality of husband and wife in the marriage relationship may be reading too much into the text, but he advanced further in that direction than any other Old Testament prophet.

The third term, "your wife by covenant," may mean that both husband and wife were members of the covenant community of Israel, or that marriage had established a covenant relationship between the two. The latter meaning seems to be the one the prophet wanted to emphasize, although the former also was true. Marriage should be regarded as a solemn covenant into which persons enter before God, the obligations of which may not be disregarded without serious consequences.

Because of the special terms that Malachi used to refer to the husband-wife relationship, one commentator has described the prophet's treatment of the subject in lofty terms: "The prophet proceeds to present the Old Testament doctrine of marriage in its highest form, pointing to its nature as a covenant relationship sanctioned by God, intended to provide for companionship and for the procreation of godly offspring."[2]

Marital problems have a profound effect on a person's spiritual life. For a man or his wife to be on good terms with the Lord when constant bickering and tension exist between them is difficult, if not impossible. First Peter 3:7 links a healthy marital relationship to an effective prayer life: "Likewise you husbands, live considerately with your wives . . . since you are joint heirs of the grace of life, in order that your prayers may not be hindered."

**God's Design for Marriage (vv. 15-16)**

In the Book of Malachi, no verses are more difficult to translate or to interpret than 2:15-16. I would propose a paraphrase of verse 15 that differs considerably in meaning from the translation that the Revised Standard Version offers. I do so because I think the paraphrase makes better sense of the verse and helps one to understand it in its larger context. The paraphrase is: *Did not God make one wife for Adam? He had power to do otherwise, had He so desired. And why did He make but one? Be-*

*"'And what does he [God] desire? Godly offspring'"* (Mal. 2:15).

*cause He was seeking a godly offspring, a purpose that would have been defeated had He given more than one wife.*

According to this interpretation, Malachi was building his case against divorce on the Genesis account of creation (Gen. 2:21-24). Christ did the same when the Pharisees questioned Him on the subject of divorce (Matt. 19:4-6).

Malachi at least alluded to the potentially harmful effects of divorce on the children who were involved. He stated that God's purpose in marriage was that one woman and one man should make a lifelong commitment to each other. Nothing short of this could provide the stable environment of love and trust that children needed in order to grow up to be godly men and women. Often, children are the most tragic victims of divorce.

A better way never has been devised to nurture a child's faith in God than in the environment of a godly home. Furthermore, the home's stability and the maturity with which the parents handle conflict and stress will affect directly the child's willingness and ability to trust the parents' God. In their day-to-day living, even in nonverbal ways, the parents are witnessing to the child. The more secure the parents are, the more secure the child will be. The more fulfilled the parents are, the more fulfilled the child will be. Ultimately, the way the parents relate to each other and to God either will block the way or will clear the way for the child to trust God. According to Malachi, God's will is that every child have the privilege of growing up in the environment of a stable, godly home.

Regrettably, this ideal is impossible to realize fully in today's society. Divorce, even among Christians, is taking place at an alarming pace. And I think that we are beginning to see the adverse effects of this on children. My wife has taught special education classes in the public school system for the past fifteen years. One year, she had a class of eight students who had acceptable IQ's but severe learning disabilities. Six of the eight were from broken homes. I wondered whether the trauma of divorce and the absence of a nurturing family had had an adverse effect on these children's ability to learn.

The troubles that lie ahead for such a divorce-ridden society as ours are difficult to predict. Joyce Huth Munro has written about the importance of childhood nurture: "Although a child may not be able to express it verbally, his family experiences tell him whether or not he is valuable; whether or not he can count on the family for support; and whether or not fellowship with God is desirable. . . . Nurturing *trust* today for mature faith later is done primarily through consistent, loving care. Mistrust develops easily from upsetting or frustrating experiences, such as making the child wait too long for physical comfort, handling him roughly, teasing him unmercifully, or departing from him suddenly."[3]

Malachi's discussion of divorce reaches its highest point in verse 16: "'For I hate divorce, says the Lord the God of Israel, and covering one's garment with violence, says the Lord of hosts. So take heed to yourselves and do not be faithless.'"

The plain meaning of this text was difficult for ancient peoples to accept, even as it is difficult for us. The Targum, the ancient Aramaic paraphrase of the Old Testament, altered it to read: "If thou hate her, divorce her." The Greek and Latin versions are similar to this. Josephus, the ancient Jewish historian, wrote: "He that desires to be divorced from his wife for any cause whatsoever, (and many such causes happen among men), let him in writing give assurance that he will never use her as his wife any more; for by this means she may be at liberty to marry another husband, although before this bill of divorce be given, she is not to be permitted so to do."[4] That Malachi's views on divorce were too high for common folk is evident, and the hardness of men's hearts led to these Aramaic, Greek, and Latin versions of the text in verse 16.

Divorce is defined further in verse 16 as "covering one's garment with violence." "Garment" usually is interpreted as a technical term that referred to the conjugal relationship. (See Deut. 22:30; Ruth 3:9; Ezek. 16:8.) According to ancient custom, a man claimed a woman as his wife by spreading his garment over her. **Violence** perhaps should be rendered *cruelty*. The prophet regarded divorce as the cruel termination of a relationship that was meant to be permanent. He called on husbands and wives to examine themselves and not to be faithless in their dealings with one another.

Malachi resisted divorce because he had such a high view of marriage. Why did he hold that divorce was wrong? His position may be summarized in four points: (1) Divorce violates a covenant that God has witnessed. (2) Divorce often brings out the worst in the marriage partners and causes them to behave cruelly and treacherously toward each other. (3) Divorce defeats God's purpose to establish the home as a place where children's lives may be shaped. (4) Because marriage is a social contract, society has to bear part of the burden for divorce. The instability of marriage undermines the stability of any society.

Therefore, God hates divorce. We also should hate it and do all we can to prevent it. At the same time, we should show love and compassion toward those who have experienced divorce, especially toward those who have been victimized by it. God hates divorce, but He still loves divorced persons. I am not sure the same could be said about all of today's people or about all of today's churches. A friend who always had gone to church told me with considerable feeling that after her divorce, she did not seem to fit in anywhere at church. Circles that had welcomed her before her divorce now were closed to her. She felt that she was being treated as an outcast. Only her stubborn determination not to give up her church saw her through. The church did not seem half as determined to try to keep her or to reach out to her.

# The Message of Malachi in Its Broader Context

This section will examine Malachi's teachings on marriage and divorce in the light of the rest of the Bible. It also will examine some of the implications for our day.

**God's Purpose in Marriage**

Some passages that define God's purpose in marriage are:

1. *Genesis 1:26-28.*—God created human beings, both male and female, in His own image. His purpose for them was that they might live together in unity, populate the earth, and exercise dominion over it.

2. *Genesis 2:18-24.*—Man in his aloneness was the only part of creation that was not "good." (See Gen. 1:31.) The fact that woman was created out of man's side emphasizes the interdependence of man and woman. Also, it stresses their independence of other social units, including the husband's parental household. An instinctive drive causes a man to leave his father's household and to be joined to his wife; thus, the two become one. What is meant in Genesis 2:24 is the personal community of man and woman in the broadest sense. It involves physical and spiritual community, mutual helpfulness and understanding, and joy and contentment in each other's company.

3. *Proverbs 5:15-19.*—This passage celebrates monogamous marriage (the marriage of one man to one woman). It is held up as a delightful alternative to sexual promiscuity and infidelity. A married man should find his sexual fulfillment in his wife alone. Then, all of their marriage will take on something of the character of an extended honeymoon.

4. *Matthew 19:4-6.*—Jesus strongly affirmed marriage by linking it to creation and to God's original intention for men and women. (See Gen. 1:27; 2:24.) In the beginning, God created both male and female and joined them together in a union that was meant to be permanent and indissoluble.

5. *Ephesians 5:21-33.*—This passage teaches that a wife should give first consideration to her husband and that a husband should give first consideration to his wife. The model for

the unity of the husband and the wife in marriage is the unity that exists between Christ and His church. (See vv. 25,32.) Admittedly, this is an ideal that people only can approximate and never can realize fully.

6. *Hebrews 13:4.*—The aim of verse 4 is to encourage chastity and fidelity to the marriage vow. In a positive way, it holds up marriage as honorable and marital intercourse as undefiled.

**The Bible and Divorce**

In examining what the Bible states about divorce and remarriage, we will look first at the Old Testament and then at the New Testament.

That divorce was practiced in Old Testament times is evident from the many regulations that governed it. (See Lev. 21:7-14; Num. 30:9; Deut. 24:1-4; Jer. 3:1-8.) Throughout the Old Testament period, divorce seems to have been undertaken only at the husband's initiative. This reflects the Old Testament perception

*"If . . . he writes her a bill of divorce . . ."* (Deut. 24:1).

of the wife as the husband's property. Indeed, a wife could be divorced if she did not please her husband or if he found some "indecency" in her (Deut. 24:1).

Only two exceptions existed to this rule. The first involved a husband who had accused his wife of not being a virgin at the time of their marriage. If a public hearing proved him to be wrong in his accusation against her, then he never could divorce her. (See Deut. 22:13-19.) The second exception was in the case of a man who had seduced or raped a virgin, in which case he was forced to marry her; and divorce was ruled out forever. (See Deut. 22:28-29.)

1. *Deuteronomy 24:1-4.*—This is the foundation passage for understanding the Old Testament position regarding divorce and remarriage. It was cast in the form of case law. It was given not as much to regulate divorce as to prevent the twice-divorced wife from returning to her first husband.

This passage does not condemn either divorce or remarriage but only the remarriage of a twice-divorced wife with her first husband. Jeremiah cited this passage as evidence that by Judah's adulterous worship of pagan gods, the nation had forfeited its legal right to return to the Lord. (See Jer. 3:1-8.) In the case of Hosea and Gomer, even though they had been divorced, he seems to have been permitted to take her back because she had not remarried. (See Hos. 1:1-3.)

Deuteronomy 24:1 permitted divorce if a wife did not find favor in her husband's eyes, or if he found some "indecency" in her. What constituted an "indecency" was the subject of heated debate among ancient rabbis. For example, Rabbi Hillel interpreted this to mean that a man could divorce his wife if she displeased him in the slightest way. The husband alone determined what constituted a displeasing act. On the other hand, Rabbi Shammai insisted that a man could not divorce his wife except for a substantial reason, such as infidelity on her part.

2. *Leviticus 21:7,14.*—In ancient Israel, a priest was not permitted to marry a woman who was divorced. This prohibition later was interpreted to include even widows, although a priest could marry the widow of another priest. (See Ezek. 44:22.) The purpose behind this regulation was to guard the priestly office's sanctity and ritual purity. It stated nothing against divorced women's remarriage to men who were not priests.

3. *Ezra 9:1 to 10:44.*—Ezra dealt harshly with the men of Jerusalem and Judah who had married foreign wives. He regarded this as a serious threat to the purity of Israel's religion and made a passionate plea for these men to put away their foreign wives. (See Ezra 10:1-5,10-11.) Thus, Ezra actually encouraged divorce for religious reasons, although Old Testament law did not require divorce in such circumstances. Certain passages even look with favor on such marriages, provided the foreign wife embraced the husband's religion. For example, Ruth the Moabitess married Boaz and became David's ancestress. Nehemiah also opposed mixed marriages, but he did not require that foreign wives and children be sent away. (See Neh. 10:30; 13:23-27.) He reminded the men of the disastrous results that Solomon's marriages with foreign women brought (13:26).

4. *Mark 10:2-12.*—Many scholars regard Mark's Gospel as our earliest source for grasping Jesus' teaching on divorce. Matthew and Luke followed Mark closely on this subject.

Mark gave Jesus' position on divorce in the context of a lead question with which the Pharisees sought to trap Him (vv. 2-4). Jesus acknowledged that Moses allowed a man to divorce his wife, provided he gave her a certificate of divorce, but He insisted that this law was given as a concession to people's hard hearts. From the beginning, God's intention had been that marriage should be permanent. Thus, Jesus acknowledged the concession to human weakness; but He flatly rejected divorce as a solution to marital problems.

Verses 10-12 clarify Jesus' teaching further. In them, He seemed to attribute more guilt to remarriage after divorce than to divorce itself. Possibly, Jesus was referring to the divorce of Herodias from her husband Philip and her remarriage to Philip's half-brother, Herod Antipas. (See Mark 6:17-20.) John the Baptist was imprisoned and beheaded because he dared to criticize this same divorce and remarriage. (See Mark 6:21-28.) He could have been saying that an easy shedding of mates for new marriage partners is an adulterous approach to marriage. Also, He injected a new teaching. The Jewish view was that a husband could commit adultery against another husband. Jesus said that husbands *and* wives could commit adultery against each other.

5. *Matthew 5:31-32.*—This passage is included in the Ser-

mon on the Mount and is almost identical to Mark 10:11-12, except that it recognizes a man's right to divorce his wife "'on the ground of unchastity.'" It also specifies that anyone who divorces his wife "'makes her an adulteress'" (v. 32). This perhaps meant that the divorced woman would be forced to remarry in order to survive economically, and thus she would be made an adulteress against her will. To lay the blame for her adultery on the men who had used and abused her would be in keeping with the general tenor of the Sermon on the Mount. In like manner, whoever married a divorced woman would be committing adultery against her first husband (v. 32*b*).

6. *Luke 16:18.*—This is almost identical to Matthew 5:31-32 except for one important difference. Matthew wrote that the man who divorced his wife caused her to be an adulteress, whereas Luke wrote that the man who divorced his wife and married another was the adulterer. Both Matthew and Luke seem to have attributed more guilt to remarriage after divorce than to divorce itself.

7. *Matthew 19:3-12.*—This passage is like Mark 10:2-12 in almost all details except that verse 9, like Matthew 5:32, allows for divorce "for unchastity." "Unchastity" seems to have been a general term that included adultery, incest, sodomy, and homosexuality.

After the Pharisees had departed, Jesus' disciples protested to Him that His views on marriage and divorce were too strict. Not to marry would be better than to have to live by His rules (v. 10)!

Jesus responded that not everyone would be able to accept His teaching and live by it (v. 11). He illustrated the difficulties some would have by pointing out that men became eunuchs (remained celibate or unmarried) for a variety of reasons (v. 12). He seemed to acknowledge that not everyone was constituted alike; for various reasons, some men would not marry. Or, Jesus might have meant that not everyone could adhere to the principle of a lifelong marriage as set forth in verses 4-6. Thus, perhaps certain persons would be capable of entering into marriage and making it work, while others would not. Jesus concluded His teaching by saying, "'He who is able to receive this, let him receive it'" (v. 12*b*).

Jesus upheld the ideal for marriage but did not fall into the

Pharisees' legalism. If this be true, we likewise should uphold the ideal that a man and his wife should live together until death parts them. At the same time, we should be more eager to show concern for divorced persons, even those who have remarried, than to judge them. The ideal, as first formulated, was not meant to increase the burden of husband or wife; it was not meant to stunt their growth and development. Rather, it was meant to provide for full self-realization in a context of mutual love and interdependence. Marriage, like the sabbath, was made for man (and woman!), and not man and woman for marriage.

8. *First Corinthians 7:10-16.*—Apparently, Paul had received an inquiry from the Corinthian church about matters related to marriage. (See 7:1.) A number of ecstatics in the church felt that their spirituality lifted them above the worldly and the physical. This led to two extremes in their behavior. Some abandoned themselves to the sins of the flesh, believing that the spirit was independent of the body and unaffected by it. Others went to the opposite extreme and became ascetics; they denied their sexual urges, even to the point of refusing to have intercourse with their spouses. Paul argued for moral purity outside marriage (v. 1) and for respect for the conjugal rights of one's spouse inside marriage (vv. 2-5).

On the matter of divorce, Paul first dealt with divorce among believers (vv. 10-11) and followed the same hard line that Jesus had laid down. Paul ruled that a wife should not separate from her husband; if she did so, she should remain single or else be reconciled to her husband. The husband was not to divorce his wife (v. 11*b*).

After Paul dealt with the question of divorce between two professing Christians, he addressed "the rest" of the cases (vv. 12-16). These were cases where one spouse was a believer and the other was not. The question was whether a believer should remain married to an unbeliever. Paul's answer was: "Sometimes, yes!" and "Sometimes, no!" If the unbelieving spouse was content to remain, then let him or her remain (vv. 12-14). But if the unbelieving spouse wished to be free of the marriage, then let that partner go free (v. 15).

Paul ended his statement with the words, "For God has called us to peace" (v. 15*b*). In this case, the guiding principle was that maintaining peace was more important than maintaining a troubled marriage. Such a marriage was not worth preserving at whatever cost. The phrase "is not bound" (v. 15) may mean that the Christian was not obligated to maintain an unviable mixed marriage. Some interpreters hold that the phrase at least implies he or she then was free to remarry, provided it was to another believer. Other interpreters insist that the phrase does not mean divorced persons can remarry.

Paul was not laying down directives that would apply to every situation; he was seeking to deal with the unique set of problems that a young church faced in a pagan environment. Today, pastors face a different set of problems. They need an extra supply of wisdom to deal with these problems.

What conclusions may we draw from the biblical texts that deal with marriage and divorce?

1. God's ideal for marriage is that two loving, caring persons should establish a union that lasts throughout life. This ideal was stated at creation; Jesus reiterated it; and Paul reinforced it.

2. Divorce is permissible for sexual infidelity, since this destroys the "one flesh" concept on which true marriage is based.

3. God's will is that estranged marriage partners be reconciled, if at all possible. Even though divorce is permissible under certain circumstances, forgiveness and reconciliation always are preferable options.

4. Remarriage of divorced persons is permitted in the Old Testament. The New Testament at least may imply that remarriage is permissible if the divorce has been caused by sexual infidelity. Remarriage in all other instances has to be undertaken without clear New Testament sanction.

5. God can forgive even the sin of adultery and can bless marriages that fall far short of the ideal. Such was David and Bathsheba's marriage. If ever a marriage violated all of God's rules, that was it! Both husband and wife were guilty of adultery. David was guilty of murder. But when David repented, God forgave him and richly blessed his marriage. David and Bathsheba were the ancestors of God's Messiah. Here is a test case that pastors should study closely as they seek to deal with problem marriages today.

**An Ounce of Prevention**

An ounce of prevention is worth a pound of cure. This proverb applies especially to an ailing marriage. What steps can marriage partners take to strengthen their marriage and to avoid becoming a part of the growing number of divorces on the modern scene?

1. Marriage partners can work at improving communication between them. One of the most frequent complaints that marriage counselors hear is: I would like to know where I stand, but I can't get him/her to talk. He/she just clams up. For a wife to try to talk to her husband if he is not willing to stop and listen is extremely difficult. For a husband to try to talk to his wife if she has tuned him out is frustrating. A hostile husband or wife may decide to punish the other by giving the partner the silent treatment. When a marriage reaches this point, it is in serious trouble. Marriage counselors contend that even bad communication is better than no communication.

2. Marriage partners can work to improve their spiritual and emotional maturity. When a marriage turns sour, it often does so because one or perhaps both of the marriage partners is acting out his/her immaturity. For spouses to be childlike is commendable; for them to be childish is devastating. Maturity is both an achievement and a gift. We are commanded to "grow in the grace and knowledge of our Lord and Savior Jesus Christ" (2 Pet. 3:18), but the capacity for growth is God's gift. Some persons function with a high level of maturity in their chosen professions only to act as rank amateurs in the business of building a home. Even pastors are not immune to this danger.

3. Marriage partners can try to accept each other's shortcomings and to be as forgiving of each other as they expect God to be of them. The duty of forgiveness begins at home. A marriage is in trouble when either of the spouses starts keeping a record of the other's faults or wrongdoings. Constant faultfinding can destroy even a good marriage.

4. If marriage problems seem to be getting out of control, couples can seek help from competent marriage counselors or ministers. Many couples drift into divorce proceedings before they really know their own minds about the matter. By then, harsh words have been spoken and harsh actions have been taken that make turning back difficult or impossible.

To have an objective, unbiased counselor sit down with the marriage partners and help them see their options and understand the implications of the actions that they are contemplating is essential. Such counselors may not try to talk the couple out of seeking a divorce. They will help the couple reach a decision about divorce in the light of the alternative possibilities and the predictable results.

5. The marriage partners can develop an intimacy that still leaves room for a certain amount of personal privacy. If husbands or wives do not wish to share every detail of their lives with each other, this does not necessarily mean that they cannot be trusted. A certain amount of privacy is necessary for emotional health and stability. Only a jealous, insecure spouse will demand a computer printout of the other's daily thoughts and activities.

6. Marriage partners can rejoice in each other's achievements and personal successes. If either receives an honor, a recognition, or a promotion, the other should be the first to offer congratulations. Competition between spouses breeds jealousy, resentment, and distrust. Let them compete with all the world, but never with each other.

7. Marriage partners can establish mutually agreed on guidelines for the nurture and discipline of their children. Discipline never should be harsh or unreasonable. It should not be out of proportion to the act of disobedience. It should be applied consistently and with the necessary follow-through, otherwise children will be given confusing signals.

Parents should not contradict each other in the discipline of children—unless abuse is involved. If they have differing views on discipline, they should discuss these when the child is not present. Otherwise, the child soon will learn to play one parent against the other. The behavioral patterns that children develop in such a situation can be disastrous for the remainder of their lives.

8. Marriage partners can be equally as polite and courteous in dealing with each other as they would be in dealing with others. Under no circumstances should they criticize, contradict, or correct each other in public. They should avoid making each other the brunt of jokes or of excessive teasing. Often, these are a smoke screen for hostility.

9. Marriage partners can learn to look on sex and sexuality as God's gifts that are intended to enhance life and enrich the marriage experience. These gifts were a vital part of the creation that from the beginning God pronounced to be "very good." (See Gen. 1:27-28,31.) Nothing evil is involved in sex and sexuality except as they are misused or abused.

10. Marriage partners can place a higher priority on cultivating nurturing, wholesome relationships within the family than on acquiring things. Many parents are so eager to acquire wealth that they are willing to sacrifice everything to achieve that end. Often, they discover that what they sacrificed is their own happiness, to say nothing of their family's happiness. What are parents profited if they enter the millionaire's circle but destroy their own family in the process?

11. Through their words and actions, marriage partners can try to raise the self-esteem of those around them. Let us observe ourselves carefully to make sure that we are not putting down our spouses or our children when they make mistakes, ask a favor, or do not live up to our expectations.

Criticisms that are spoken even in a casual way can cause permanent harm to the persons who are closest to us. Do we ever use such statements as the following? You're so clumsy! Sometimes I honestly think you don't have good sense! You never do anything right! I've never seen a child as hard-headed as you! You're so lazy it hurts! If I were you, I'd be ashamed to be seen in public! With grades like that, you never are going to amount to anything! I hate you when you act like that! I'm ashamed for people to know that you are my son (or daughter)! Look at all I've done for you!

Ask yourself: How would I feel if someone spoke to me like that? The proven fact is that people either live up to or live down to the expectations that others have of them.

12. Marriage partners can work to make home a place to which family members love to return. A home should be a haven of rest in a harried world, an island of sanity in a sea of madness. A home should be a refuge into which family members can enter to weather life's storms and to gather strength to engage life's continuing challenges. Let it be a place of good books, music, flowers, laughter, and, above all, love. For those who have shared in such a home, all the way to heaven is heaven.

**Children and Divorce**

Recent studies of the effects of divorce on children have shown that in divorce, children always suffer. They are the victims who are hurt most severely.

Some of the symptoms that have been observed in children of divorced parents are these:

1. a high incidence of depression and sadness
2. guilt over the divorce and an uneasy feeling that they may have caused it
3. a refusal to accept the finality of the divorce and a clinging to the hope that the parents will reconcile
4. bodily pains and distresses
5. a tendency to exhibit attention-getting behavior that clashes with the rules of society—truancy, running away, deliquency, poor school performance, sexual misbehavior, drug use, temper tantrums, and aggression
6. difficulty in resolving normal childhood and adolescent conflicts
7. a tendency to withdraw into one's own private world
8. a fear of forming relationships of intimacy and trust, lest they be hurt again
9. fear of abandonment
10. hurt and disappointment that their parents did not love them enough to stay together
11. a fear of their own failure as marriage partners.

A husband and a wife who are marriage counselors tell about a brother and a sister who appeared together in juvenile court, each charged with habitual truancy from school. Each had a lawyer and a supervising probation officer seated nearby. The presiding judge convened the court and asked if the children's parents were present. One of the probation officers explained that their parents had been notified but that they were divorced. Notices had been sent to them, but they had been too busy to come to this or to the previous hearing.

The two children were on the verge of tears, for despite the lawyers' and the probation officers' presence, they felt that no one cared what happened to them. They felt unloved, abandoned, and alone.

The counselors said this about the probable future of these two children: "The major victim of divorce is the child. If a prediction were to be made on the future of the two children described above, it would be that the girl might continue a pattern of truancy, drop out of school, . . . develop sexual relationships on a casual level . . . to get the feeling of love that was lacking at home. She may marry while still a teenager, . . . have one or more children in order to be needed and . . . view life as a drudgery, . . . see herself as a 'nobody' because, after all, she was not worth very much or her parents would have cared. . . .

"The boy might continue a pattern of truancy, be caught stealing a car in which he is joyriding, be sent to Juvenile Hall repeatedly, and leave school untrained, to go from job to job without steady employment. He may take drugs to feel a part of his peer group, commit petty thefts or burglaries, and end up in the county jail. With a criminal record, his jobs will be only an unskilled type. He may marry while still a teenager, have children at an early age, and view his children as 'nobodies,' just as he was viewed."[5]

Of course, many children from broken homes have grown up to be successful and well-adjusted adults. But if the situation that was just described occurred only occasionally, it still would be a terrible price for children to have to pay for their parents' failure. I suspect that it occurs more frequently than we would like to believe. Many of us could supply names and faces to the two children who were described. Indeed, children are the major victims of divorce.

Children often become unwilling pawns in a divorce suit as battling parents use them to get back at each other. The wealthier the parents are and the greater access they have to lawyers, the more likely such battles will be long and especially bitter. The child who is caught in the middle may be harmed beyond repair by such fighting. No matter how the court finally rules, it will be a no-win solution for the child. Jesus' words especially seem to be appropriate to a situation like this: "'Whoever causes one of these little ones who believe in me to sin, it would be better for him if a great millstone were hung round his neck and he were thrown into the sea'" (Mark 9:42).

The One who said, "'Let the children come to me, do not hinder them'" (Mark 10:14), still looks with compassion on the helpless victims of divorce. No doubt they are special subjects of His concern, and must be of ours.

# Lessons for Life from Malachi 2:10-16

*The acid test of our religion is how we relate to other persons.*—The two places where relationships become most important are the church and the home. Our responsibility to the first is to promote its fellowship and to do all that we can to strengthen its unity. Our responsibility to the second is to relate to our spouses and our children in such a way that our homes become a stable environment of love and trust.

*The marriage covenant has God as its witness, and anyone who deals treacherously with a trusting spouse must answer to Him.*—The Bible has no reference to a religious ceremony accompanying marriage, but even without such a ceremony those entering into marriage were responsible to God to do everything possible to make the marriage succeed.

*Marital problems have a profound effect on the spiritual life of everyone involved.*—For a family to have a healthy spiritual atmosphere when constant tension exists between the husband and the wife is difficult, if not impossible.

*God's ideal for marriage is that one woman and one man make a commitment to each other for life.*—This ideal was not formulated to increase the burden of either husband or wife but to provide for full self-realization in a context of love and trust. Those who make this ideal their own discover the deeper sense of fulfillment in marriage that God intended from the beginning.

*A better way to nurture a child's faith than in the environment of a stable, godly home never has been devised.*—The stability of the home and the maturity with which the parents relate to each other will affect directly the child's readiness and ability to relate to the parents' God. In their day-to-day living, even in nonverbal ways, parents are witnessing to their faith and are making the child's having a faith of his or her own either simpler or more difficult.

*Situations arise where maintaining peace becomes more important than maintaining a troubled marriage.*—Some marriages clearly are not made in heaven, and last-minute efforts cannot alter the situation. Sometimes, Christians marry undesirable persons thinking that the persons will reform after marriage. This seldom happens. Such marriages may not be worth preserving at whatever cost. Sometimes, divorce seems to be the lesser of two evils.

*Often, children are the most tragic victims of a divorce situation.*—We should be more sensitive to the hurts that children feel when divorce takes place. In many ways, divorce is worse than a death, because at least they could feel that a dead parent still loved them. But a parent who leaves them, often without warning, signals to them a lack of love and a lack of concern. Is it any wonder that they respond in anger and frustration? No one has a right to inflict such hurt on another human being, much less on a child!

*We should uphold the divine ideal for a lifelong union in marriage but at the same time minister lovingly to those in whose lives this ideal has been shattered.*—We all live "east of Eden," outside the land of innocence and perfection. As we minister to one another in such a context, the most that we ever can do is to mount a salvage operation. Fortunately, our God is in the business of salvaging broken lives and mending broken relationships. He can bless marriages that are less than ideal and can do good through persons who are trying to make a new beginning. Such a recognition of the way He works opens the door to helpful ministry.

---

1. From *The New English Bible*. Copyright © The Delegates of the Oxford University Press and the Syndics of the Cambridge University Press, 1961, 1970. Reprinted by permission. Subsequent quotations are marked NEB.
2. James H. Gailey, Jr., "The Book of Malachi," *The Layman's Bible Commentary* (Richmond: John Knox Press, 1962), 15:138.
3. "The Family: Cradle of Spiritual Development," *Review and Expositor*, LXXV, 1 (Winter, 1978), p. 51.
4. Josephus, *Antiquities*, Book IV, Ch. 8, p. 273.
5. T. Roger Duncan and Darlene Duncan, *You're Divorced But Your Children Aren't*, The Transformation Series, (Englewood Cliffs, N.J.: Prentice-Hall, Inc., 1979), pp. 9-10.

# Personal Learning Activities

1. To stress his people's unity and distinct identity, Malachi reminded them that they had ____________ and ____________. (Choose the correct answers from the list.)
   (1) The Scriptures (3) A rich heritage (5) Tradition
   (2) The Temple (4) One God (6) One Father
2. According to Dr. Page Kelley, when Malachi condemned marriage with "the daughter of a foreign god," he meant marriage with an idolatress. ___True ___False
3. Malachi was the only Old Testament prophet to deal with the problem of ____________ in detail.
4. According to Dr. Page Kelley, marriage should be regarded as a ____________. (Choose the correct answer from the list.)
   (1) Contract (3) Covenant
   (2) Convenience (4) Legal agreement
5. Who are the major victims of divorce?

Answers: 1. (4), (6); 2. True; 3. Divorce; 4. (3); 5. The children.

# 4 Where Is the God of Justice?

2:17 to 3:5

Malachi must have had difficulty believing his ears. He heard his fellow Israelites complaining that God was showing favoritism to evildoers and was giving the righteous people the short end of the deal. Furthermore, they said, God was not concerned about seeing that justice was done on earth. In their eyes, He had become a do-nothing God. (See 2:17.)

Malachi responded by announcing an approaching judgment. The great and terrible day of the Lord was about to break on the people's heads. After a forerunner had been sent to prepare the way, the Lord would come suddenly to His Temple. (See 3:1.) His appearing would answer critics and would silence complainers once and for all.

Sinners would not be able to endure the day of the Lord's coming or stand when He appeared, for He would be like a refiner's fire and like fullers' soap. (See 3:2.) Israel's dross would be burned away by the refining fire, and its impurities would be removed by the strong soap of judgment.

The process of refining and purifying would have special significance for the Levitical priests. Malachi previously had accused them of abusing their priestly responsibilities. The situation had become so serious that their sacrifices no longer were acceptable to the Lord. (See 1:6-8,12-14.) Malachi hoped that the day of judgment would purify the priests and would enable them once more to offer sacrifices that were pleasing to the Lord. (See 3:3-4.)

Another segment of society also would be affected by the day of judgment. This included sorcerers, adulterers, false swearers, and all oppressors of the community's weaker members. (See 3:5.) Against those who had committed such evils, the Lord would rise up as Judge, Witness, and Prosecutor. Their punishment would be swift and decisive.

# The Necessity for Judgment (2:17)

Let us review briefly what had brought about the situation Malachi faced. He was called to prophesy during one of the most difficult periods in Israel's history.

First, the time was one of deferred hopes and delayed promises. The prophets before Malachi had predicted that the Lord would return in glory to His Temple. (See Ezek. 43:2-4; Hag. 1:8.) However, although the Temple had been rebuilt for more than half a century, no sign of the Lord's return had occurred. The prophets also had predicted that the Lord would bless the land with prosperity (see Hag. 2:6-9; Zech. 8:9-13), but the people still found themselves the victims of relentless poverty. Their situation was so desperate that some of them had been forced to sell their children into slavery. (See Neh. 5:1-5.) Unemployment was widespread throughout the land, for "there was no wage for man or any wage for beast" (Zech. 8:10).

Second, the time was one of continuing oppression for the struggling community in Jerusalem. The prophets had foretold Israel's triumph over its foes (see Isa. 60:10-14; 61:5-6), but instead the foes continued to have the upper hand. The Persians still ruled the land with an iron fist and were destined to do so for about another century and a quarter. The already poor people had to dig even deeper into their meager resources to pay tribute to Persia and to furnish provisions for the Persian soldiers who were stationed in the land. (See Neh. 5:15.)

As if this were not enough, the Jews' hostile neighbors were putting pressure on them from all sides. Earlier, the hated Samaritans had succeeded in delaying the reconstruction of the Temple. (See Ezra 4:4-16.) They used every kind of tactic to keep Nehemiah from rebuilding Jerusalem's walls. (See Neh. 4:1-9; 6:1-9.) The Edomites also became a thorn in Israel's side. They took advantage of the Exile to seize Judah's territory that stretched south from Jerusalem. For this reason, the returning Exiles had difficulty regaining a foothold in the land. Hatred for the Edomites burned within them.

Third, Malachi lived at a time when injustice and oppression were widespread throughout the Jewish community. Unscrupulous Israelites had no qualms about exploiting their own countrymen. The poor were charged exorbitant rates of interest and were faced with foreclosure if they fell behind with their payments. (See Neh. 5:1-5.) The rich and powerful exploited the especially vulnerable—hired laborers, widows, orphans, and resident aliens. (See Mal. 3:5.) These merchants of misery lived by the principle of the survival of the slickest. Some persons managed to enrich themselves at the expense of the poor and needy.

Fourth, Malachi's age was one of religious skepticism and indifference. A half-century of poverty and oppression had produced a dangerous reaction on the part of the Jews. The Jews' faith of former days had given way to doubts concerning God's goodness and justice. A new temper controlled the Jewish mind, and many persons had begun to sit "in the seat of scoffers" (Ps. 1:1). The land was ripe for judgment.

When Malachi stood up to announce the imminent arrival of the day of judgment, he began by accusing the people of having wearied the Lord with their words. (See 2:17*a*.) The prophet shared the Old Testament view of the power and importance of speech. (See also 3:13-18.) Speech always has been a reliable gauge to a person's character and personality. In a profound sense, we are what our speech reveals us to be.

Some persons boast of being plain-spoken and blunt, even to the point of being rude and offensive to others. Their philosophy seems to be: If you think it, you might as well say it! The problem with such a philosophy is that spoken words take on an existence all their own. Once thoughts are expressed in words, they never can be recalled. They go on either blessing or cursing, depending on their content. If this is true of the words that we speak of one another, how much more is it true of the words we speak of God?

Perhaps the importance and impact of words explains why two of the Ten Commandments relate to speech. One forbids taking God's name in vain (Ex. 20:7); the other forbids bearing false witness against a neighbor (Ex. 20:16).

With our tongues, we can do great good. We can use them to witness to God's love. We can sing of His grace. We can encourage the downhearted. Through the spoken and written word, we can extend our ministries far beyond ourselves.

But with our tongues, we also can do great harm. A word that is spoken carelessly or in anger can wound others and can bring reproach on God. The wrong use of the tongue can cancel the good that we might otherwise want to do. The Book of James reminds us the tongue is capable both of great good and of great evil. (See Jas. 3:10-12.) Whether its influence will be positive or negative will be determined by the control we exercise over it.

Malachi used a bold figure of speech when he accused his people of having wearied the Lord with their words. Elsewhere, the Bible affirms that the infinitely great and wise Lord never faints or grows weary. (See Isa. 40:28.)

How, then, can God's people be said to weary Him sometimes? The answer seems to be that they are capable of wearying Him through their sin and disobedience. In and of Himself, He never grows weary. But His people's rebellious spirits can have this effect on Him. Long ago, He said to the Israelites: "But you have burdened me with your sins, you have wearied me with your iniquities" (Isa. 43:24*b*).

Have we, too, burdened and wearied the Lord through our sins and iniquities? Have we done this as individuals? Can we think of ways our churches or our denomination may have done this? The possibility that we may have wearied our Lord should be enough to send us to our knees in confession and repentance. Such a response on our part would go a long way toward resolving the problems in our personal lives, in our churches, and in our denomination.

In Malachi's day, the people made their customary response to the prophet's charge that they had wearied the Lord. They exclaimed: "'How have we wearied him?'" (2:17). They responded as if they were unaware of wrongdoing. They pretended not to know what the prophet meant by his accusation. They had fallen so deeply into sin that they did not even know that they were sinful. They were quick to find fault with God but slow to recognize their glaring faults. Persons of this mentality seldom change. They have made up their minds and do not want to be confused with facts.

Even so, the prophet proceeded to answer the people's question just as if they sincerely had requested information and counsel. He pointed out three ways they had wearied the Lord with their words.

First, the people had said: "'Every one who does evil is good in the sight of the Lord'" (2:17*b*). This was a serious charge, for it meant that the Lord could not distinguish between the righteous persons and the wicked individuals. In other words, He was lacking in moral discernment. This was similar to Isaiah's earlier charge against the sinners in Judah: "Woe to those who call evil good and good evil, who put darkness for light and light for darkness, who put bitter for sweet and sweet for bitter!" (Isa. 5:20). Malachi's listeners were charging God with this same kind of spiritual blindness. Little did they realize that they, not God, could not distinguish between right and wrong. Our human nature tends to blame someone else for our faults rather than to shoulder our responsibility. (See Gen. 3:11-13.)

Second, the people of Malachi's day were accusing God of taking delight in evildoers. (See 2:17c.) By this accusation, they meant that He preferred evil persons' company to that of good persons. To take delight in someone also means to bestow favors and blessings on that person. Thus, the men and women of Malachi's audience were accusing God of showing partiality to the wicked people when He distributed His gifts. (See also 3:15.) This was the same as declaring that God was evil, not good. To imagine a more blasphemous charge than this would be difficult.

Some people might object that other Old Testament prophets and saints had made similar complaints against God. Did not Jeremiah protest to the Lord that He had favored the wicked persons over the righteous individuals? (See Jer. 12:1-2.) Had not Habakkuk accused the Lord of doing nothing in the face of repeated cries for help against violent men? (See Hab. 1:1-4.) And what about Job? He accused the Lord of delivering the earth into wicked men's hands and of blinding its judges' eyes. (See Job. 9:24; 21:29-33.) And Israel's psalmist confessed that he envied the arrogant persons when he saw the prosperity they enjoyed and the ease with which they lived. (See Ps. 73:3-14.)

An unmistakable similarity is evident between the complaints other Old Testament persons voiced and the complaints of the people whom Malachi condemned. If we were to look for the difference between the two, we doubtless would find it in the spirit in which the complaints were made. In the one instance, they were sincere cries for help that arose out of a sense of perplexity, confusion, and hurt. In the other instance, the complaints were shouts of rebellion that were motivated by a spirit of pride and arrogance. The people of Malachi's day had set themselves up to judge God. Their attitude was one of open hostility. Surely, God knows how to distinguish between sincere protests against earth's injustices and rebellious persons' arrogant cries.

The third offending word that the Jews spoke against God was in the form of a question. They asked: "'Where is the God of justice?'" The question was not designed to obtain information about God's whereabouts but to launch a complaint against Him. The answer that the Jews expected was that the God of justice was nowhere to be found. As far as they were concerned, He was an absentee God who was totally unconcerned about administering justice in the world. In the face of life's inequities and injustices, He simply had abdicated His responsibility. Like their forefathers who had put God to the test at Massah, the Jews of Malachi's day were demanding to know: "'Is the Lord among us or not?'" (Ex. 17:7).

At the heart of the third complaint was a denial that God was involved actively in the affairs of history. He was regarded as being outside history and indifferent to what went on within it. Of course, nothing could be further from the view of God that the Bible presents. In the Old Testament and the New Testament, He is pictured as working at the center of history and guiding it toward its ultimate goal. He steadfastly refuses to leave its final outcome in wicked people's hands. Therefore, to deny His active involvement in history is to deny His existence.

## Preparation for the Lord's Appearing (3:1)

"'Behold, I send my messenger to prepare the way before me!'" With these words, the Lord announced the coming of a forerunner to prepare the way before Him. "Behold" is a strong word. Whenever a prophet used this word to introduce an announcement, he did so in order to stress its urgency and the certainty of its fulfillment.

Sending a messenger to prepare the way before the Lord refers to an ancient custom that was related to kings' travels. Whenever a king wanted to journey to some distant part of his realm, he would send a trusted servant to prepare the way before him. The servant would arrange for workers to build a roadway through mountains and forests and over dangerous streams. The king's highway had to be smoothed and leveled, and all obstacles to safe travel had to be cleared away. Nothing was to be allowed to hinder the king's progress or to endanger his safety.

The forerunner's further responsibility was to announce the king's coming and to provide an appropriate welcome for him. Thus, the forerunner had to assure the king of a safe journey and of a fitting reception wherever he traveled.

Malachi's prediction of a forerunner to prepare the way before the Lord calls to mind a similar passage in Isaiah 40:3-5: "A voice cries: 'In the wilderness prepare the way of the Lord, make straight in the desert a highway for our God. Every valley shall be lifted up, and every mountain and hill be made low; the uneven ground shall become level, and the rough places a plain. And the glory of the Lord shall be revealed, and all flesh shall see it together, for the mouth of the Lord has spoken.'"

Malachi's announcement of a forerunner's coming, to be followed shortly by the Lord's appearance, was in direct response to those who had asked contemptuously: "'Where is the God of justice?'" (2:17). Malachi warned that they would find out soon enough. The God of justice was coming to visit them, and it would be a visit they never would forget.

The forerunner theme is expanded in 4:5-6, where he is identified as "'Elijah the prophet'" (4:5). This theme played an important part in Jewish and Christian theology.

How are we to identify the messenger who would be sent to prepare the way before the Lord? Some have taken him to be Malachi, since the Hebrew form ***malachi,*** *my messenger,* is found in 3:1 and in 1:1. According to this view, Malachi saw his task to be that of preparing the way for the Lord's coming in judgment. However, that Malachi later would have referred to himself as "'Elijah the prophet'" is hardly likely. (See 4:5-6.) Since both "Elijah" and the "messenger" were sent to herald the coming day of judgment, the prophet must have understood them as the same person. Thus, the notion that he was Malachi has not gained wide acceptance.

The New Testament is our best guide to the Christian interpretation of the forerunner. There, he is identified consistently as John the Baptist. John was seen as the messenger who was sent to prepare the way before Christ. To understand how any Christian interpreter could deny that Malachi's prophecy was fulfilled in John the Baptist is difficult.

Yet, some interpreters claim that this prophecy awaits its fulfillment at the final judgment. They argue that Malachi's prophecy was fulfilled only partially in John the Baptist's ministry. In their view, its final fulfillment will come when Elijah reappears in person at the final judgment.

Orthodox Jews still expect Elijah to reappear in order to usher in the messianic age. A place is set for him at each Passover meal, for the Jews believe that his return will coincide with the celebration of the Passover festival. A door is left ajar somewhere in the house to make certain that he is not turned away. Since most Jews do not accept Jesus as their Messiah, they have no reason to regard John the Baptist as fulfilling the prophecy about Elijah.

However, Jesus warned His disciples not to expect Elijah's literal return. (See Matt. 17:10-13.) In the light of His clear teaching, we probably should regard Malachi's prophecy as having been fulfilled in John the Baptist's mission and in the terrible period of judgment that ended in Jerusalem's destruction in AD 70. No other fulfillment seems to be necessary.

Malachi declared that once the forerunner had finished his work, the Lord would come to His Temple suddenly. (See 3:1.) The Hebrew word translated **suddenly** means *unexpectedly*. Compare the statement in 3:1 with the statement in 3:5 that the Lord would be a "swift witness" against the ungodly individuals among His people.

In 3:1, the Lord is designated further as "'the messenger of the covenant.'" This should not be confused with "my messenger" in the earlier part of the verse. Since **messenger of the covenant** just as easily could be translated *angel of the covenant*, some interpreters have taken this to refer to the angel of the Lord. Elsewhere in the Old Testament, the angel of the Lord is synonymous with the Lord.

The Lord who was coming to His Temple is pictured as being

sought by the people. He is called "'the Lord whom you seek'" and "'the messenger of the covenant in whom you delight.'" These probably were words of sarcasm. Indeed, the people were asking: "'Where is the God of justice?'" (2:17). But their question was asked in derision. They were not seeking Him sincerely; they really did not want to find Him. They were more like the people described in Amos 5:18-20. They wanted the day of the Lord to come but were ignorant of its devastating effects on them. The modern parallel would be Christians who talk much about Christ's second coming but who would be ill-prepared to meet Him if He should appear suddenly. Christians who are prepared to meet the Lord do not have to brag about it all the time.

The Temple was designated as the place where the Lord would make known His presence to His people. Why would He come to the Temple? At least two interpretations are possible. In the first place, Malachi may have intended to say that judgment would begin at the Temple. This would have fitted in with his earlier accusations against the priests and the Levites. A similar warning is in 1 Peter 4:17*a*: "For the time has come for judgment to begin with the household of God."

The second interpretation has to do with the Old Testament concept of God's tabernacling presence among His people. This concept had a positive and a negative side. On the positive side, it meant that the Lord manifested His approval of His people when He sent His glory to dwell in their midst. On the negative side, it meant that He showed His strongest disapproval of them when He withdrew His glory from them.

The glory of the Lord is mentioned first in the Bible in connection with the Exodus from Egypt. (See Ex. 16:7,10; 24:16-17.) When Moses asked to see God's glory, God told him that such a vision was too much for human sight. (See Ex. 33:18-23.)

*Glory* could be applied to human beings and to God. When it was used of human beings, it referred to their honor, prestige, reputation, and wealth. When it was used with reference to God, it described His majesty, power, and holiness. Whenever God's glory manifested itself, it took the form of a bright light or a burning fire. It might be hidden by a cloud or by smoke in order to shield the beholders' eyes from its blinding brightness.

Thus, the glory of the Lord functioned in a dual role: It revealed God, and it concealed Him. It revealed all of Him that human eyes could behold. At the same time, it bore eloquent testimony to the fact that the celestial vision was more than human eyes could take in. The normal response of those who saw the revelation of God's glory was to cover their eyes and to fall on their faces.

The Lord usually manifested His glory in the central sanctuary. The glory first came to dwell in the tabernacle that was constructed in the wilderness. (See Ex. 40:34-35.) This symbolized the Lord's pleasure with His people and His abiding presence in their midst. However, in the days of Eli, the Lord became displeased with His people and allowed the Philistines to capture the ark of the covenant in battle. (See 1 Sam. 4:11.) This symbolized the Lord's departure from His people. Eli's daughter-in-law graphically expressed this realization by naming her newborn son *Ichabod*. For her, the name meant "'the glory has departed from Israel.'" (See 1 Sam. 4:10-11,19-22.) This certainly was one of the darkest hours that the ancient Israelites ever experienced.

However, the picture brightened again when Solomon built a permanent sanctuary to house the ark of the covenant. In the account of Solomon's dedicating the Temple, note the words: "And when the priests came out of the holy place, a cloud filled the house of the Lord, so that the priests could not stand to minister because of the cloud; for the glory of the Lord filled the house of the Lord" (1 Kings 8:10-11). The return of the Lord's glory was a sure sign that He had bestowed His favor on His people.

Israel's history had a tragic way of repeating itself. Just before the destruction of Jerusalem in 587/586 BC, Ezekiel was granted a vision of the Lord's glory departing once more from the Lord's Temple. (See Ezek. 8—11.) The abominations that were being committed in the city were so serious the Lord was being driven from the midst of His people. (See Ezek. 8:6.) Reluctantly, He withdrew from the Temple and from the city. First, the glory proceeded from the holy of holies to the threshold of the Temple, where it rested for a while. (See Ezek. 9:3; 10:4.) Then, it moved from the threshold to the east gate of the Temple, where it stopped once more. (See Ezek. 10:18-19.) Finally, the glory withdrew altogether and stood on the mountain east of the city. (See Ezek. 11:22-23.) Its departure meant that both the Temple and Jerusalem were doomed to destruction. The destruction came in 587/586 BC. Jerusalem, like Shiloh before it, had become Ichabod. The glory had departed.

Ezekiel not only prophesied the departure of the Lord's glory from the Temple, but he also was given a vision of its return in future days. His vision of hope was expressed in these words: "Afterward he brought me to the gate, the gate facing east. And behold, the glory of the God of Israel came from the east; and the sound of his coming was like the sound of many waters; and the earth shone with his glory. And the vision I saw was like the vision which I had seen when he came to destroy the city, and like the vision which I had seen by the river Chebar; and I fell upon my face. As the glory of the Lord entered the temple by the gate facing east, the Spirit lifted me up, and brought me into the inner court; and behold, the glory of the Lord filled the temple" (Ezek. 43:1-6).

Unfortunately, the people of Malachi's day did not believe that the glory of the Lord had returned to the restored Temple. They lived with the lingering fear that the Temple still was forsaken by the Lord. They had rebuilt the Temple, but only the Lord could endow it with His presence. They believed five things that had been in Solomon's Temple were missing from the second Temple. These were the ark of the covenant; the fire on the altar; the glory (also called the *Shekinah*); the Holy Spirit; and the sacred lots, the urim and thummim.[1]

The foregoing discussion may help to explain why Malachi's listeners were seeking the Lord and eagerly awaiting His return to the Temple. They longed for the day when the Lord's house no longer would be without the Lord's presence. This suggests that Malachi's announcement may have contained a note of promise and of hope that the Lord would come suddenly to His Temple. Many people must have interpreted the prophet's words as a signal for great rejoicing. Their long-deferred hopes were about to be fulfilled.

What about us and our churches? Has the glory of the Lord departed? What name would describe us best? Would it be Immanuel, "God with us?" Or would it be Ichabod, "the glory has departed?"

A friend who grew up in another state shared this true story with me. His parents took him to church regularly on Sunday. On the way to their church, they passed an abandoned church in a field beside the road. One day, he asked his parents why the church no longer was used. They explained to him that it once had been a thriving country church. Then one day, a family of foreigners moved into the community and began to attend services at this church. Some members welcomed them, but many were offended by their presence. At the next business meeting, the matter was brought up; and the church voted by a sizeable majority to ask the foreign family not to attend any more church services. Then, my friend's parents explained that from that time the church began to die. Its membership dwindled until it finally had to close its doors. The glory had departed. The church was dead.

Of course, not all dead churches close their doors. The church in ancient Sardis fitted this category. John wrote concerning it: "'"I know your works; you have the name of being alive, and you are dead"'" (Rev. 3:1).

When Jesus said, "Upon this rock I will build my church, and the gates of hell shall not prevail against it" (Matt. 16:18, KJV), He did not mean that a disobedient church is insured against failure. Churches can die; and often, they do die. A church is invincible only as long as it follows the path of faithful obedience and crossbearing.

When Paul was addressing the Corinthian Christians on the subject of speaking in tongues, he used the occasion to describe what ought to happen when unbelievers come to church services. He wrote: "If, therefore, the whole church assembles and all speak in tongues, and outsiders or unbelievers enter, will they not say that you are mad? But if all prophesy, and an unbeliever or outsider enters, he is convicted by all, he is called to account by all, the secrets of his heart are disclosed; and so, falling on his face, he will worship God and declare that God is really among you" (1 Cor. 14:23-25).

Is God really present in our churches? Are unbelievers impressed by this fact when they attend church services with us? If we do not expect to encounter God when we attend worship, then something is wrong. If we seek Him with all of our hearts, He will come to us and abide with us. Then, our witness will be more effective as outsiders note that God is truly in our midst. Then we will have become the "Immanuel" church, not the "Ichabod" church.

## The Purpose Behind Judgment (3:2-4)

"But who can endure the day of his coming, and who can stand when he appears?" (3:2). With these words, Malachi warned his listeners against a superficial view of the day of the Lord. Apparently, they were inclined to regard it as a gala occasion. They thought it meant that the Lord would return to His Temple in all of His glory and make them the recipients of all His blessings. They looked on the day of the Lord as a painless path to a bright future.

Malachi had an entirely different view of what the day of the Lord would be like. He must have shocked the people when he implied that few would be able to endure the day of the Lord's coming or to stand when He appeared.

The day of the Lord is a term that was used widely in the Old Testament, especially in the prophetic books. Sometimes, reference is made to it simply as "the day" (see Ezek. 7:10,12), or as "that day." (See Isa. 2:11-12; Amos 8:3,9; 9:11.) These references are not as much to literal days as to the various times and seasons in history when God intervenes to judge the wicked individuals and to deliver the righteous persons.

The day of the Lord may vary in its design and purpose from one prophet to another. As Isaiah used it in the eighth century BC, it referred to the devastation of Judah by the Assyrians. (See Isa. 7:17-20.) Ezekiel, who wrote more than a century later, applied it to the destruction of the nations by the king of Babylon. (See Ezek. 30:3-4,10.) These testing times were looked on as days of the Lord, and references were made to many others. (See Joel 2:1-2; Amos 5:18-20; Zeph. 1:14-18.) Christians have interpreted Malachi's references to the day of the Lord as pointing to the events that surrounded John the Baptist's birth, Jesus' coming, and Jerusalem's destruction in AD 70.

What was the Lord's purpose in bringing a day of judgment on His people? First, He would come as a refiner's fire to burn away all of their dross (Mal. 3:2*b*).

Fire often was used in the Old Testament as a metaphor of God's presence among His people. He appeared to Moses in a flame of fire out of the midst of a bush. (See Ex. 3:2.) He guided the Israelites during their journey through the wilderness with a pillar of cloud by day and a pillar of fire by night. (See Ex. 13:21-22.) He descended on Mount Sinai in fire and smoke. (See Ex. 19:18.) Later, as Moses warned the Israelites not to offend God by making graven images, he said to them: "For the Lord your God is a devouring fire, a jealous God" (Deut. 4:24; see also Heb. 12:29).

Note that fire serves a double purpose. It destroys, but it also purifies. Its destructive power is stressed in a number of passages that deal with the theme of judgment. The psalmist wrote about God's judgment: "Fire goes before him, and burns up his adversaries. . . . The mountains melt like wax before the Lord,

*"'He is like a refiner's fire'"* (*Mal. 3:2*).

before the Lord of all the earth" (Ps. 97:3,5). Isaiah described God's coming to judge the nations in similar terms: "'For behold, the Lord will come in fire, and his chariots like the stormwind, to render his anger in fury, and his rebuke with flames of fire. For by fire will the Lord execute judgment, and by his sword, upon all flesh; and those slain by the Lord shall be many'" (Isa. 66:15-16). Nahum also wrote of the destructive side of judgment in words similar to Malachi's: "Who can stand before his indignation? Who can endure the heat of his anger? His wrath is poured out like fire, and the rocks are broken asunder by him" (Nah. 1:6). The sobering truth is that unrepentant sinners have reason to dread God's judgment. (See Heb. 10:26-27.)

But what can we say about fire's purifying effects? Certainly, the refiner's fire—the metaphor that Malachi used—was meant to suggest refining and purifying. Silver and gold are of little value unless they have passed through the refiner's fire. Fire burns away the impurities but leaves the precious metals in a more workable state. Proverbs 25:4 testifies to the positive effects of refining: "Take away the dross from the silver, and the smith has material for a vessel."

What is true of metals is true of individuals and of nations. We cannot render acceptable service to God if our lives have not been refined and purified. The Lord rejected Jerusalem because its silver had become dross and its wine had been diluted with water. (See Isa. 1:21-22.)

Isaiah's call to be a prophet furnishes a good example of an individual who was purified by fire. Isaiah's vision of the Lord seated on His throne and surrounded by choirs of seraphim singing praises to His holiness filled the prophet with great fear and dread. (See Isa. 6:1-8.) He cried out that he was lost, a man of unclean lips, who was unworthy to live in the presence of such awesome holiness. Then one of the seraphim came to him bearing a coal of fire from the burning altar and pressed it against his lips. The prophet's lips were cleansed, his sins were burned away, and he was prepared for effective service. When he heard the Lord calling for a volunteer, he responded: "'Here am I! Send me.'" God had taken care of Isaiah's past; He also could have his future.

But what about the fiery trials that sometimes fall across our pathways? Does God still permit His children to pass through the refiner's fire? A word of caution is needed as we seek to answer these questions. We must avoid the temptation to seek easy answers to a complicated problem. An answer that fits one situation may not fit another. Many mysteries remain about human suffering that we cannot understand.

At the same time, the Bible teaches that God sometimes allows suffering and trials to overtake His servants in order that they may be purified and prepared for more effective service. Paul's "thorn in the flesh" was a good example of this kind of suffering. It taught him to rely more on God and less on himself. (See 2 Cor. 12:7-9.) Paul also wrote the church at Philippi that the trials he had endured in a Roman prison had advanced the gospel. (See Phil. 1:12-14.)

The trials that God allows His children to endure must not be interpreted as a denial of His love for them. In some circumstances, the trials may be seen as proof of His love. James wrote to Christians who faced heavy trials: "Count it all joy, my brethren, when you meet various trials, for you know that the testing of your faith produces steadfastness. And let steadfastness have its full effect, that you may be perfect and complete, lacking in nothing" (Jas. 1:2-4).

Peter wrote in a similar vein and offered encouragement: "In this you rejoice, though now for a little while you may have to suffer various trials, so that the genuineness of your faith, more precious than gold which though perishable is tested by fire, may redound to praise and glory and honor at the revelation of Jesus Christ" (1 Pet. 1:6-7).

The author of Hebrews went a step further when he affirmed that suffering as discipline gives proof that God loves us and accepts us as His children. Concerning the intended outcome of such suffering, he wrote: "But he [God] disciplines us for our good, that we may share his holiness. For the moment all discipline seems painful rather than pleasant; later it yields the peaceful fruit of righteousness to those who have been trained by it" (Heb. 12:10*b*-11).

Fire burns! Suffering hurts! Nevertheless, God continues to work all things together for good—even including suffering—for all who love Him and are responsive to His will. (See Rom. 8:28.) The psalmist witnessed to the positive power of suffering:

"Bless our God, O peoples, let the sound of his praise be heard, who has kept us among the living, and has not let our feet slip. For thou, O God, hast tested us; thou hast tried us as silver is tried. Thou didst bring us into the net; thou didst lay affliction on our loins; thou didst let men ride over our heads; we went through fire and through water; yet thou hast brought us forth to a spacious place" (Ps. 66:8-12). In a more recent time, the unknown author of "How Firm a Foundation" ("K" in Rippon's *Selection of hymns*) expressed this truth in similar words:

> "When thro' fiery trials thy pathway shall lie,
> My grace, all-sufficient, shall be thy supply;
> The flame shall not hurt thee, I only design
> Thy dross to consume, and thy gold to refine."

During my student days. H. H. Rowley spoke in seminary chapel and told the following story. A British sea captain used to go out into the North Sea to fish for mackerel. Since this was before the days of refrigeration, he had to dump his fish in holding tanks and try to keep them alive until he could return to market. Invariably, however, some of the fish would die on the return trip and would have to be thrown overboard.

One day, the captain snagged a small shark in one of his nets and had to dump it into the tank along with the other fish. The shark chased the other fish and kept them stirred up throughout the remainder of the voyage. When the captain arrived back in port, however, he made an interesting discovery. Not a single dead fish was found in the holding tank. The mackerel had been kept so busy avoiding the shark that they had not had time to die!

Does God sometimes put a shark in our tank? Does He allow us to be refined by fire and tested by adversity? And may such experiences not be evidence of His love for us and of His concern for our growth and spiritual development? That certainly was His purpose for Israel as Malachi defined it.

For the good of His people, God came as "a refiner's fire' " and as " 'fullers' soap' " (3:2*b*). The metaphor of fullers' soap is equally as powerful as that of the refiner's fire. "Fuller" was an ancient term that was used to describe someone who laundered clothes by hand. The soap that fullers used in biblical times was prepared with lye obtained from the ashes of certain plants that grew in the salt marshes along the shores of the Dead Sea. Even in our country, lye soap commonly was made from the potash that had been leached out of the ashes of certain types of wood. Such soap was tough on the hands, but it was most effective in removing dirt and stains from clothing.

God's purpose in judgment not only was to burn away the dross of sin but also to wash away its filthy stains. The process of refining and cleansing was designed especially for "'the sons of Levi'" (Mal. 3:3), a term that included all of the Temple priests and attendants. These proud leaders must have resented Malachi's suggestion that they needed to be refined by fire and washed with laundry soap. Spiritual leaders often have shown a tendency to be blind to their own faults. The Pharisees were a prime example of this, and people of their spirit still live among us.

The priests needed to have their sins removed so that they could offer acceptable sacrifices to the Lord (3:3-4). "'Right offerings'" (v. 3*b*) signify offerings that conform to God's standards. Earlier, the prophet had condemned the priests for violating these standards (1:6-8).

*"'He is like . . . fuller's soap'" (Mal. 3:2).*

The prophet looked forward to a time when Israel's sacrifices again would be pleasing to the Lord, "'as in the days of old and as in former years'" (v. 4). Perhaps this referred to the time of the first Temple. Malachi often called on the people to return to the pure religion of their ancestors. (See 2:5-6; 4:6.)

One commentator has described the refining and cleansing that would make such a return possible: "The refiner is beautifully represented as coming and sitting down beside the crucible, that the fire may not be too hot, or the process left incomplete. He bends in patient love over the furnace until . . . when he looks down on the liquid metal he can see his own image perfectly reflected there; then the process is completed, and the fire removed."[2]

In every age, God's goal for His servants is that they should offer acceptable worship to Him. When does this take place? The answer is given in Romans 12:1-2: "I appeal to you therefore, brethren, by the mercies of God, to present your bodies as a living sacrifice, holy and acceptable to God, which is your spiritual worship. Do not be conformed to this world but be transformed by the renewal of your mind, that you may prove what is the will of God, what is good and acceptable and perfect." No acceptable worship is possible apart from full commitment to Him who is the object of our worship. Anything else is only sham and pretense.

## A Day of Reckoning (3:5)

The impression that one gains from verse 5 is that a showdown was about to take place between God and those who had broken His covenant. Phrases such as "'draw near,'" "'judgment,'" and "'witness'" suggest a court scene. It was a court scene in which God would act as Judge, Witness, and Prosecutor. He would be "'a swift witness'" against evil-doers, which suggests that He already knew the facts of the case and did not need to spend time gathering evidence. His speed and haste in judging would be an effective response to those who had accused Him of being negligent in executing justice. (See 2:17*b*.) Those who had accused Him of injustice now must stand trial for their own injustices.

Who were the guilty persons who had to stand trial before the divine Judge? First on the list were the sorcerers. All forms of sorcery and witchcraft were strictly off limits to God's people. (See Ex. 22:18; Deut. 18:10-14; 2 Chron. 33:6; Micah 5:12.) Present-day forms of these forbidden practices include satan worship, the serious consulting of horoscopes, fortune-telling, attempts to communicate with the dead, and various other forms of magic. God's people have no need for these works of darkness. All of the benefits that these black arts promise people are not to be compared with the blessings that believers receive through Bible study, prayer, and fellowship with the Lord.

The second group of people that was singled out for punishment were the adulterers. In the Old Testament, adultery is interpreted as having sexual relations with a married woman. It was regarded as violating the marital rights of the woman's husband. The law against adultery (see Ex. 20:14) was based on the premise that marriage was sacred and that its sanctity was to be respected by outsiders. A sin as serious as adultery could not escape God's judgment. Adulterers are included with the immoral persons and the idolaters as among those who cannot enter God's kingdom. (See 1 Cor. 6:9-10.) Adulterers either must repent and seek forgiveness or else must face Him who is both Judge and Prosecutor. This warning is needed as sorely today as it was in Malachi's time.

The third group that was to be judged were the people who swore falsely. To swear falsely meant to give false testimony under oath. What was at stake was the judicial system's integrity. False testimony robbed people of the right to a fair trial. This sin also was considered serious enough to be condemned by one of the Commandments. (See Ex. 20:16.)

A fourth group that the divine Judge would condemn was anyone who practiced injustice. This included all who tried to better their own lot at the expense of society's helpless members, such as the hired worker, the widow, the orphan, and the resident alien. The indictment against the perpetrators of injustice was that they had kept back the hired hands' wages, had oppressed widows and orphans, and had violated the rights of foreigners who lived in their midst.

The charges of injustice have a familiar ring in our day. A

warning similar to Malachi's is in the Book of James: "Come now, you rich, weep and howl for the miseries that are coming upon you. Your riches have rotted and your garments are moth-eaten. Your gold and silver have rusted, and their rust will be evidence against you and will eat your flesh like fire. You have laid up treasure for the last days. Behold, the wages of the laborers who mowed your fields, which you kept back by fraud, cry out; and the cries of the harvesters have reached the ears of the Lord of hosts. You have lived on the earth in luxury and in pleasure; you have fattened your hearts in a day of slaughter. You have condemned, you have killed the righteous man; he does not resist you" (Jas. 5:1-6).

In defending the poor and the oppressed persons' rights, Malachi was subscribing to the same high ideal for justice that one finds in prophets like Isaiah (see Isa. 1:11-17), Amos (see Amos 5:21-24), and Micah (see Mic. 6:6-8). These prophets understood justice to be the norm that God required of all His people. It meant that one be honest, fair, and impartial toward all other

*"'I will be a swift witness . . . against those who oppress . . .'" (Mal. 3:5).*

persons. God wanted justice to be established throughout the earth (see Isa. 42:4), and nothing ultimately will be able to prevent Him from reaching that goal.

The Roman symbol for justice was a blindfolded goddess holding a pair of scales in her right hand. The scales were balanced perfectly, which indicated that in its ideal state justice was blind and impartial either to one side or to the other. It favored neither rich nor poor, high nor low, king nor peasant.

However, a significant difference existed between the Roman model for justice and that presented in the Old Testament. According to the Hebrew model, justice involved a deep-seated and fundamental bias in favor of the poor and the oppressed persons. Since these often were the victims of ruthless persons' power and greed, and since they had no one to defend their cause, God became their special defender, their redeemer-kinsman.

According to the Hebrew model, justice was not blind; it was clear sighted. It might be represented as a clear-eyed prophet who held the scales of judgment in one hand. With the forefinger of the other hand, he pressed down on the side of those whom earth's justice had ignored. "Help of the helpless" and "friend of the friendless" are more than just lovely sounding phrases. They accurately describe God's relationship to all who are downtrodden and abused.

The final group that the Lord condemned consisted of people who did not fear Him. This was the most serious charge against the people of Israel. To fear the Lord meant to regard Him with respect and reverence, and to obey His Commandments. The Jews' lack of such reverence and obedience was the wellspring of all the other crimes with which they had been charged. When people no longer fear God, they lose all incentive for right living and decent conduct.

A clear parallel exists between Israel's situation and ours. Because so many of our citizens do not fear and worship God, our land is overrun with superstition, immorality, greed, violence, and injustice. To deal with these problems one by one merely is to treat the symptoms and to ignore the root of the matter. No lasting improvement will be made in our situation until we experience a radical turning to God. Will you pray that such a turning may take place soon?

# Lessons for Life from Malachi 2:17 to 3:5

*For Christians to speak carelessly or irreverently about the Lord is a serious sin.*—Words are an accurate index to character. We will be judged by our words. Kind, true, and loving words will bring the Lord's approval. Harsh, false, and irreverent words will bring His condemnation.

*We can weary the Lord through our sin and disobedience.*—We need to make sure that we do not abuse God's patience.

*Those who seek the Lord in a merely superficial way will not find Him.*—The people whom Malachi addressed were seeking the Lord (3:1), but only in a superficial way. In order to find Him, we must seek Him with all of our hearts.

*The glory of the Lord was revealed to Israel in the tabernacle and in the Temple; however, it has been revealed to us in Christ.*—The New Testament describes the Lord's glory as tabernacling in our midst through the incarnation: "And the Word became flesh and dwelt among us, full of grace and truth; we have beheld his glory, glory as of the only Son from the Father" (John 1:14). When the church lives for His glory, it honors Him and draws people to Him.

*Nothing is consumed in the fires of judgment except sin.*—Therefore, Christians have nothing to dread or fear when God allows trials to come their way. They can be confident that none of these things can separate them from God's love in Christ Jesus. (See Rom. 8:35-39.) The fires of judgment are not meant to destroy them but to take away their dross. Christians' trials are not a denial of God's love for them but a proof of that love.

*Persons who continue to rebel against the Lord must face His wrath on the day of judgment.*—He will come as Judge, Witness, and Prosecutor, even as Malachi foretold. A day of reckoning will come for all people who have despised Him and have resisted His will. The opportunity to repent must be seized now.

---

1. See R. E. Clements, *God and Temple* (Philadelphia: Fortress Press, 1965), pp. 123-126.
2. T. V. Moore, *The Prophets of the Restoration* (New York: Robert Carter and Brothers, 1856), p. 380.

# Personal Learning Activities

1. The people to whom Malachi ministered were facing (choose the correct answers from the list):
   ___(1) Unfulfilled hopes
   ___(2) Poverty
   ___(3) Persian control
   ___(4) Hostile neighbors
   ___(5) Internal injustice
   ___(6) Religious indifference
2. Malachi said that the people had ___________ God with their words. (Select the proper response from the list.)
   (1) Honored
   (2) Praised
   (3) Pleased
   (4) Wearied
3. Malachi said that God would send His messenger, later identified as ___________, to prepare for God's coming in judgment.
4. Where would the Lord make His presence known to the people?
5. The Lord would come in judgment as a refiner's fire and as a warrior's sword. ___True ___False
6. The showdown between God and those who had broken His covenant is described in terms of ___________________.

Answers: 1. (1),(2),(3),(4),(5),(6); 2. (4); 3. Elijah; 4. In the Temple; 5. False; 6. A courtroom scene.

# 5 How Shall We Return?

Malachi 3:6-12 is perhaps the best-known passage in the book. The Jews had forfeited God's blessings by failing to bring their tithes and offerings to the Temple treasury. The prophet challenged them to resume tithing. He promised them that if they would do so, God would open the windows of heaven and pour out His blessings on them. The emphasis on tithing makes these words well-known to Baptists. Many stewardship sermons have been preached from this passage.

However, what often has been overlooked—even by the ablest commentators—is that Malachi set tithing in the larger context of repentance. What made the Israelites' withholding their tithes of such consequence was that it was a symptom of a far more serious wrong: their unwillingness to repent and to return to God. Faithfulness in stewardship always must be seen as one of the fruits of repentance and as an indication of the depth of a person's commitment to God.

When the average churchgoer hears the subject of stewardship mentioned, likely he or she will think that it refers to the annual campaign to subscribe the church budget. Many persons regard stewardship as little more than a well-organized effort to secure generous pledges from rather reluctant givers. Uncooperative church members sometimes are given an ultimatum on Commitment Sunday: "If you do not turn in your pledge today, someone from the finance committee will pay you a visit." This threat usually gets the job done. The budget is subscribed, and the members breathe a sigh of relief. They will not have to think seriously about stewardship for another year.

The threaten-type concept of stewardship is different from what the Bible reflects. Faithfulness in stewardship is not making a pledge once a year in order to get the finance committee off your back. It is not even tithing one's income, if by so doing tithers think that they are free to use the balance of their income without reference to God's will. In fact, if one's concept of stewardship involves only gifts of money—whether the gifts are great or small—it has not begun to approach the biblical concept. The Bible requires that stewards be faithful and trustworthy. (See 1 Cor. 4:2.) This involves faithfulness in using all of life's gifts and resources and not simply in managing money.

To promote church giving without setting it in the larger context of repentance and faith-commitment to God actually may do more harm than good. While such promotion may help to raise the church budget, the danger is that it will pressure people into giving for the wrong reasons. In the end, it may produce a kind of works-righteousness that denies the adequacy of the cross and fosters a spirit of Pharisaism. This is why Malachi's corrective is needed today.

## A Nation of Backsliders (3:6-7*a*)

Possibly, someone in Malachi's audience blamed Israel's troubles on God's being unpredictable. The person may have complained that God changed His attitude toward Israel so often that no one could be sure what He was going to do next. Would He bless the nation or curse it? The complainer said that people had no way of knowing. The charge was that God was unpredictable, and the Israelites were not to blame if they could not understand His ways or meet His demands.

The Lord's response was that He had not changed (v. 6*a*). This is only one of many Old Testament texts affirming the fact that Israel's God was changeless. The psalmist expressed the same truth: "Of old thou didst lay the foundation of the earth, and the heavens are the work of thy hands. They will perish, but thou dost endure; they will all wear out like a garment. Thou changest them like raiment, and they pass away; but thou art the same, and thy years have no end" (Ps. 102:25-27). The psalmist must have received great assurance to know that his God never would change and never would grow old. Only God's changeless nature gives meaning and stability to the changing human scene.

Because God had not changed, the faithless Jews had not been consumed (v. 6*b*). God's patience and longsuffering toward sinful Israel were stressed. If He had been disposed to do so, He could have blotted the nation off the earth. The Hebrew word translated "consumed" usually described total annihilation. (See Job 4:9; Ps. 37:20; Isa. 1:28.)

But why had God spared such a sinful people? His doing so certainly was not because they had changed. Rather, He spared them because He remained a God of love and compassion, even in the face of their rebellion. In other words, He did so because of the kind of God He was, "a God ready to forgive, gracious and merciful, slow to anger and abounding in steadfast love" (Neh. 9:17*b*; see also Ex. 34:6-7). God's nature is to be gracious; to punish always is His "alien . . . work" (Isa. 28:21).

The Jews deserved to be punished. Whereas the Lord had been constant in His compassion toward them, they had been constant in their rebellion against Him. The Greek version of verse 6*b* reads: "But ye, the sons of Jacob, have not refrained from the iniquities of your fathers." They were called "sons of Jacob" because they were like Jacob. Following the example that he set, they had lived by deceit and treachery. This theme is developed further in verse 7.

According to verse 7*a*, the people were guilty of chronic backsliding: "'From the days of your fathers you have turned aside from my statutes and have not kept them.'" God's statutes were the laws and ordinances that He had given to guide Israel in right living. For the nation deliberately to turn aside from these meant that it had abandoned a path that was well-marked. I once heard George Ernest Wright, a leading Old Testament scholar, say that the only covenant Israel ever knew was a broken covenant, broken by the people's flagrant disobedience even while Moses was on the mount of revelation. (See Ex. 32:1-35.) Except for God's infinite patience and compassion, the nation would have been rejected from the beginning.

## An Invitation to Repentance (3:7*b*)

The Lord extended a gracious invitation to the prodigal nation to come back to Him: "'Return to me, and I will return to you, says the Lord of hosts'" (v. 7*b*).

The Hebrew word translated "return" is the Old Testament word that commonly was used to describe repentance. Repentance takes place when a person who is going away from God makes an about-face and comes back to Him. This was what God wanted Israel to do. He wanted the nation to turn away from evil and to turn toward Him in penitence and trust.

God's invitation was accompanied by a promise. "'Return to me,'" He said, "'and I will return to you.'" Perhaps, the prophet understood Israel's failure to repent as being responsible for the Lord's delay in returning in glory to His Temple. (See the discussion on 3:1.) He was not free to return to them as long as they refused to return to Him. (See Isa. 59:1-2.) The New Testament contains a similar invitation to those who have wandered away from God: "Draw near to God and he will draw near to you" (Jas. 4:8*a*). God always comes to meet the penitent sinner who turns to Him. Jesus likened God's attitude to that of a father welcoming home his lost son. (See Luke 15:20-24.) Oh, the grace and compassion of our Heavenly Father! The observation has been made that absolutely nothing you or I ever could do will cause Him to love us any more than He already does.

In response to God's invitation to return to Him, the people asked: "'"How shall we return?"'" (v. 7*b*). Their question is similar to the one in Micah 6:6, though not as sincere. The people were not asking for instructions about how to return to God. The basic meaning of their question was: *What need have we to repent?* They were ignorant of any wrongdoing; thus, they were unwilling to accept responsibility for their predicament. They manifested the same spirit as the Pharisees and the scribes who criticized Jesus for associating with sinners. (See Luke 15:1-12; 18:9-14.) The people's denial of guilt paved the way for Malachi's charge that they were guilty of having robbed God.

## A Nation of Robbers (3:8-9)

The Lord answered the people's denial of any wrongdoing on their part with a question: "'Will man rob God?'" (v. 8). The Hebrew word translated **rob** is found in only two places in the

Old Testament: in this passage and in Proverbs 22:23. It means *to defraud another person or to take something forcibly from that person.*

The Greek translation of Malachi 3:8 is: "Will a man insult God?" The Greek translator used a verb that meant to lift up the heel, to trip another, a verb from which the name Jacob was derived. **Jacob** was a *heel grabber* and a *supplanter*. The Greek translation suggests that Malachi's question might be: "Will a man 'jacob' God?" That is, will a man dare to treat God the way Jacob treated those about him, always cheating and robbing to improve his own situation?

When the prophet asked if a man would rob God, the people probably answered with a resounding No! Such a possibility was too shocking even to be given serious consideration. To rob people would be bad enough, but to rob God would be unthinkable. They indignantly denied the charge and asked for proof that they had committed such a horrible crime.

Malachi responded that the people had become a nation of robbers by withholding their tithes and offerings from the Lord. Again, to consult the Greek text is helpful. It reads: "in that the tithes and the first-fruits are with you still." This implies that the worshipers were taking the offerings that should have been given to God and using them for their own benefit. Perhaps they justified their action with the excuse that times were hard and they needed all that their land could produce. In other words, they could not afford to be faithful stewards in a time like that. Have you ever heard people use this excuse to justify withholding their tithes and offerings?

A few years ago, a middle-aged man was converted in the church where I was pastor. In his newfound joy of salvation, he decided to begin tithing. However, he felt that he could not afford to do so until he had paid some outstanding debts and had put his financial affairs in order. The result was that he never got around to tithing. He died without experiencing the joy that might have been his.

Tithing was an ancient and widespread custom. The Egyptians, Babylonians, Assyrians, and Canaanites practiced it even before Israel became a nation. The Old Testament records that Abraham offered Melchizedek a tithe of the booty he had gained in warfare. (See Gen. 14:18-20.) Elsewhere in the Bible, the tithe always consisted of the produce of the soil. Offering the tithes of the crops and of the herds acknowledged that ultimately, God owned the land and that the Israelites were only His tenants.

Considerable attention has been given to the question of which law of the tithe was in effect when Malachi wrote. Deuteronomy 12:5-7; 14:22-29; 26:12-15 provided that an annual tithe of all the soil's produce should be brought to the central sanctuary and eaten there by the tither, the members of his household, and the Levites. Those who lived a great distance from the sanctuary were permitted to sell the tithe in their hometown, take the proceeds of the sale to the central sanctuary, and there purchase whatever was necessary for the shared feast. (See Deut. 14:24-27.) Every third year, the tithe was handled in a different way. Instead of being brought to the central sanctuary, it was laid up in the various towns across the country. Then, it was distributed to the Levites, the sojourners, the fatherless, and the widows. (See Deut. 14:28-29; 26:12-13.) Therefore, the tithe in Deuteronomy served several different purposes. First, it was an offering that acknowledged God's ownership of the soil and all of its produce. Second, it reinforced the prayer that God would continue to bless His people with abundant crops. (See Deut. 26:15.) Third, it was a means of support for the Levites, who otherwise would have had no portion or inheritance among the people. (See Deut. 12:12; 14:27,29*a*.) Finally, it was one of the earliest-known attempts to establish a poverty program to benefit the sojourners, the fatherless, and the widows in Israel. (See Deut. 14:29*b*; 26:12-13.)

Leviticus 27:30-33 and Numbers 18:21-28 placed a different emphasis on tithing. These passages specified that the whole tithe should be brought to the central sanctuary and presented to the Levites. (See Num. 18:21-24.) In turn, the Levites were commanded to pay a tithe of the tithe to the priests. (See Num. 18:25-28.) This concept of giving has come to be known as "storehouse giving." It emphasizes giving as a means of support for the sanctuary (church/denomination) and its priesthood (pastor/staff) rather than for more general, charitable purposes. It also gives the offerers less freedom in deciding how their tithe is to be used.

In ancient Israel, storehouse giving seems to have received

greater stress after the Exile. The reasons for this are not hard to find. The Temple worship no longer was under the patronage of Israel's kings. It had to be supported entirely by the people's freewill offerings. Storage rooms, perhaps similar to those uncovered at Masada and at other sites in Palestine, were built alongside the Temple. These contained rows upon rows of clay jars in which oil, wine, grains, and dried fruits could be stored for the future needs of the Temple and its personnel. By bringing their tithes and offerings to the storehouse, the people acknowledged their responsibility to maintain the Temple and its priesthood, as well as the Levitical singers and the Temple custodians.

The Temple storehouses certainly existed in Nehemiah's time (445 BC). He described a situation in which one of the large storage chambers had been misused by one of the priests. (See Neh. 13:4-9.) When Nehemiah discovered that the storehouses were empty and that the Levites and singers were not being supported by the people's tithes, he took decisive action to correct the situation. (See Neh. 13:10-13.)

Malachi also must be interpreted against the background of the people's failure to tithe. He called on them to bring their *full* tithes to the storehouse in order that God's house might have food in it. (See Mal. 3:10.) The full tithes were to be desposited in the Temple in order that those who ministered before the Lord might be supported adequately. Note that the prophet who previously had been so critical of the priests (see Mal. 1:6-14; 2:1-9) now was concerned about their welfare.

**Offerings** (Mal. 3:8) comes from a Hebrew word that means *to be raised up, lifted up,* or *exalted*. In about half of this word's occurrences in the Old Testament, it is rendered "heave offering" or "wave offering." This usually refers to the portion of a sacrificial offering that was assigned to the priests for their use. (See Lev. 7:30-34.) Apparently, the priest lifted it up and swung it toward the altar; then, he may have waved it away from the altar. In one form of the offering, it was taken from the priest and burned on the altar. The waving of the sacrificial portion was a ceremonial act that indicated the priest first had offered it to God and then had received it back from Him.

Malachi's use of the term translated "offering" may have indicated his further concern for maintaining the priesthood through the people's gifts. Wave offerings and tithes are linked together again in 2 Chronicles 31:12, which the King James Version reproduces as "the offerings and the tithes," and in Nehemiah 10:37, which is rendered "our offerings . . . and the tithes of our ground" (KJV). Interestingly, in both passages the concern also is with providing adequate maintenance for the priests and the Levites. These are further examples of storehouse giving.

In the Jewish literature from the interbiblical period, frequent reference was made to the tithe. The Mishnaic tract "Seeds" gives minute instructions for tithing all foodstuffs that grew from the soil. In the Book of Tobit, a pious Jew—Tobit—is pictured as saying: "I used to hurry off to Jerusalem with the firstfruits of crops and herds, the tithes of the cattle, and the first shearings of the sheep; and I gave them to the priests of Aaron's line for the altar, and the tithe of wine, corn, olive oil, pomegranates and other fruits to the Levites ministering in Jerusalem" (Tobit 1:6-7; NEB[1]). The Book of Judith refers to the tithes of wine and oil as being "dedicated and reserved for the priests who stand in attendance before our God in Jerusalem" (Judith 11:13; NEB[2]). The Book of Ecclesiasticus exhorts the worshiper: "Be generous in your worship of the Lord and present the firstfruits of your labour in full measure. Give all your gifts cheerfully and be glad to dedicate your tithe. Give to the Most High as he has given to you, as generously as you can afford. For the Lord always repays; you will be repaid seven times over" (Ecclesiasticus 35:8-11; NEB[3]). These references are important because they describe the Jewish attitude toward tithing in the pre-New Testament period.

Tithing rarely is mentioned in the New Testament. References are made in only four passages: Matthew 23:23; Luke 11:42; 18:12; and Hebrews 7:1-10. The first two, Matthew 23:23 and Luke 11:42, are parallel accounts of the same saying. They represent our Lord's condemning the scribes and the Pharisees for emphasizing tithing garden herbs, such as mint, dill, and cummin, more than performing the law's weightier matters, such as justice, mercy, and faith. The other Gospel reference to tithing is in Luke's account of the parable of the Pharisee and the tax collector who went up to the Temple to pray. In his prayer, the Pharisee boasted that he gave tithes of all that he got (Luke

18:12). The final New Testament reference to tithing is in Hebrews 7:1-10. The writer argued that because Abraham, Levi's ancestor, paid tithes to Melchizedek, the priesthood of Christ, who is a priest after the order of Melchizedek, is superior to that of the Levitical priests.

The fact that the New Testament never specifically commands Christians to tithe raises a number of questions. Was tithing required only of the Jews in the Old Testament period? To what extent are we justified in insisting that tithing is a Christian obligation? I have wrestled a great deal with these questions in trying to understand Christ's claims on my own life. Other Christians may come to a different answer, but I have concluded that for us to speak of the "law" of the tithe as still "binding" on Christians is wrong. I think that to do so is wrong for at least two reasons. First, it reactivates a part of the law from which Christ has set us free. (See Gal. 2:15-16; 5:1.) Second, it makes obedience to Christ a response of law and not a response of love. The tithe is not "a ten-per-cent income tax." Rather, it is a gift that we freely offer to God—our expression of gratitude for His bountiful goodness to us. God loves cheerful givers, not grumpy givers. (See 2 Cor. 9:7.)

At the same time, let me hasten to stress that I believe in tithing as a model for voluntary Christian giving. I think of it like this: If faithful Jews could offer a tithe of their income to God, how can Christians afford to do less?

Tithing is a suitable model for our giving for several reasons. First, it is not demanded of us like a law; therefore, it is *voluntary giving*. Second, it is *reverent giving*, for it acknowledges God as the Lord of all the earth and the One who gives us the power to get wealth. (See Deut. 8:18.) Third, it is *regular giving*; it spares us constantly having to decide whether to give and how much to give. Fourth, it is *proportionate giving* that enables us to give as God has prospered us. (See 1 Cor. 16:2.)

I was living with my parents on a small farm in southern Alabama when I felt called to the ministry. My father was a tenant farmer, and we had little to live on. I realized that if I was going to be a minister, I needed to go to college. But where was I to get the money to do so?

I decided to sell whatever I could and use the money to enroll in Howard College in Birmingham, Alabama. The only problem was that I did not have much to sell—only a bicycle that I had used on a paper route and a registered Jersey heifer I had raised from a calf. The sale of both netted me only about eighty dollars.

My last day at home before I set out for college was a Sunday. As I sat in church that day, I decided that I ought to tithe the money I had received in order to express my gratitude and commitment to God. The treasurer in the little church opened my envelope and tried to return the money to me. He argued that I needed it more than the church did and that I should keep it for my college expenses. What he failed to realize was that giving the money was far more important to me than keeping it. Since then, I have given larger gifts; but I never have given one that brought me more lasting joy and satisfaction. It was a small price to pay for such a tremendous blessing.

Malachi 3:9 begins: **You are cursed with a curse.** These words mean *to be cursed indeed*. The Old Testament pictured a cursed man as one for whom nothing went right. His whole life fell to pieces. The precise effects of the curse that Malachi announced are not stated, but the following verses indicate that they included droughts, poor crops, and locust plagues. The "whole nation" was condemned. The word used for **nation** is ***goy,*** a word normally used to refer to Gentiles. When Israel was addressed as a ***goy,*** it usually was within the context of judgment and condemnation. (See Deut. 32:28; Judg. 2:20; Isa. 1:4; Jer. 5:9.) This certainly was not a complimentary way for Malachi to refer to his people.

## God's Gracious Offer (3:10-12)

As we read 3:10-12, we must remind ourselves that it is set in the context of a call to repentance. (See v. 7.) In this passage, tithing is singled out as an evidence of repentance. Whenever God's people have a repentant spirit, they will give generously and spontaneously. However, we need to remember that for Malachi giving the tithe was only the earnest of repentance; it was not the full act of repentance. We never can buy our way into God's favor. True repentance involves a radical reorienting of life, a turning away from evil and a turning toward God. A generous spirit is one evidence that such an experience is genuine.

The close relationship between tithing and farming was especially evident in God's gracious offer to bless His people. In response to their faithful tithing, He promised to send copious showers on their fields (v. 10) and to destroy the devouring locusts that might threaten their growing crops (v. 11). Their prosperity would be so abundant that all nations would rise up and call them blessed (v. 12).

God began by challenging His people to bring the "full tithes" into the storehouse (v. 10). What is stressed is our need to commit fully our possessions to God. The whole earth belongs to Him. Like the ancient Israelites, we are only God's tenants and must give an account for our use of His gifts. We came into the world with nothing; we will leave it with nothing. We really do not "own" anything. Our possessions merely are borrowed. An old man in Kentucky often was heard to say, "I never saw a U-Haul behind a hearse!"

D. T. Niles has given a clear statement of the commitment that is required of Christian stewards: "It is irresponsible . . . to think that Christians can find time and money and strength for everything that everybody else does, and that with spare money in spare time with spare strength they can serve the ends of God's Kingdom. The great pearl is bought only by selling small pearls (Matt. 13:45-46). Where no pearl has been sold, there obedience to the demand of the Kingdom has not begun."[4]

On one occasion in David's career as Israel's king, he wanted to build an altar to the Lord on the site of a threshing floor that belonged to a man named Araunah. He negotiated with Araunah to buy the threshing floor. In an outburst of generosity, Araunah offered to give the threshing floor to the king and also to provide the oxen and the wood for the king's burnt offering. (See 2 Sam. 24:18-25.) The king resolutely refused to accept the gift. He said, "'No, but I will buy it of you for a price; I will not offer burnt offerings to the Lord my God which cost me nothing'" (v. 24). What a difference would be made in our lives if all of us would come to the place where we could say, "I will not offer to the Lord my God that which costs me nothing." What do you think would happen if we made this the rule by which we measured all of our service to God?

Today, fewer and fewer Americans make their living by cultivating the soil. For most of us, stewardship involves our use of what we receive as profits, wages, and salaries. Still, reason exists for us to stop and to take stock of the effect that our way of life is having on the earth's environment. A vital part of our stewardship responsibility is to make wise use of the earth's resources and to hand them on to future generations.

Unfortunately, our record in stewardship of the earth's resources is not too encouraging. Too often, we have squandered those resources and have polluted the air and water. The results of our selfishness and recklessness are beginning to come home to us.

This past spring, my wife and I were returning from Washington, D.C., to Louisville by automobile. Just outside Washington, we decided to take the Skyline Drive that overlooks the beautiful Shenandoah Valley. We had driven this route several years earlier, and we remembered the beautiful trees and the forests of rhododendron bushes with their spring colors. However, this time we were in for a great disappointment. The trees and shrubs were green enough at the lower levels; but once we had climbed to an elevation exceeding three-thousand feet, we had the impression that we were entering a war-devastated landscape. The trees and shrubs either were dead or dying. Stately trees stood like skeletons against the sky. No grass grew beneath them. The soil seemed sterile and dead. After we had driven several miles through this mountainous wasteland, we returned to the main highway. We were saddened by what we had seen, and we also were somewhat alarmed. We could not help asking ourselves: Are these mountains trying to tell us something? How much longer before even the valleys will not support plant life? Do you not agree that part of Christian stewardship is for us to do all we can to protect our environment? How can God fulfill His promise to bless us if we do not do our part?

Through Malachi, God exhorted His people to bring their tithes to the storehouse (3:10). The storehouse was adjacent to the Temple. It is described in Nehemiah 13:5 as "a large chamber where they had previously put the cereal offering, the frankincense, the vessels, and the tithes of grain, wine, and oil, which were given by commandment to the Levites, singers, and gatekeepers, and the contributions for the priests." This is what earlier was called "storehouse giving," the modern equivalent of which would be channeling one's gifts and contributions through a local church.

Should Christians restrict their giving to the causes that their local churches sponsor? This is a difficult question to answer, but I want to suggest some guidelines that may help us to clarify our thinking about this matter.

1. I think that to say we should give our tithes through our churches is biblically sound.

2. I think our churches are responsible for being good stewards of the gifts that the people bring. For a church to be selfish and extravagant is just as sinful as for its members to be so.

3. I think causes exist which Christians should support over and above their gifts to their churches. In the city where I live, an annual Crusade for Children is conducted that enjoys widespread community support.

4. We must not neglect our own families' needs (see 1 Tim. 5:8), and especially our aged parents' needs. Jesus condemned the scribes and the Pharisees for using their "storehouse giving" as an excuse not to attend to their parents' needs. (See Matt. 15:3-6.)

5. We should be prepared to respond to acute needs that suddenly confront us. On several occasions in my lifetime, I have come face-to-face with someone in desperate need and have felt constrained to do what I could to meet the need. I always have been blessed when I did so. Let us take care lest we pass up an opportunity to be good Samaritans.

6. I think we should exercise great caution in giving to persons who make public appeals for contributions but who are not publicly accountable for the manner in which they use these contributions. Many—but certainly not all—of the television evangelists fall in this category. As Southern Baptists, we can support many of the same causes that these evangelists champion and do it much more effectively through our own mission boards and agencies.

The Lord challenged the Jews to prove Him—put Him to the test—with their tithes (v. 10). He was asking them to prove the bountifulness of His ability to bless. We must exercise caution in interpreting words like these. The question we have to ask is:

To what extent does the passage justify our putting God to the test today?

Often, the Bible records that God tested certain persons. However, it warns people against putting God to the test.

How are we to understand God's challenge to the Jews to put Him to the test in the light of the prohibition against doing this? Ralph L. Smith, professor of Old Testament, Southwestern Baptist Theological Seminary, Fort Worth, Texas, has suggested one possible answer: "It may be that this passage in Malachi should be understood as a one-time, special act on God's part to renew the fires of faith in an age of skepticism and indifference."[5] Also, God may not want us to test Him by rash or evil deeds to see if He will punish us, but He may want to encourage us to test Him by acts of obedience to see if indeed He will not bless us. In any event, we need to listen to Smith's words of caution: "We cannot presume upon God's goodness. We can test him only when he invites us. There is a great danger in testing God when our hearts are not right (Mal. 3:15)."[6] We should remember that Jesus refused to test God simply to prove that He was the Son of God (Matt. 4:7).

The Lord's readiness to bless faithful tithers was expressed in a bold metaphor. He promised to open the "windows of heaven" and pour out on them an unlimited blessing (v. 10). For "windows of heaven," the Septuagint (Greek) version reads "cataracts [torrents] of heaven." Ancient Hebrews conceived of the windows of heaven as openings set in the firmament of the heavens. They believed that God controlled the earth's supply of rainfall by opening and closing these windows. (See Gen. 1:7; 7:11; 8:2; 2 Kings 7:2,19.) What God promised through Malachi was an abundant supply of rainfall for the farmers who were faithful in tithing their crops. This was a fitting reward for tithing, since tithing acknowledged God's ownership of the land on which the farmers grew their crops.

Through Malachi, God stated clearly the promised blessing's unlimited nature. God would continue to empty out His blessings on the people until, according to the Hebrew's literal sense, "an absence of a sufficiency" existed. The Septuagint reads: "until ye are satisfied." The Targum (an Aramaic paraphrase) reads: "until you say, 'Enough!'" The difficulty with interpreting this promise is in determining whether the "sufficiency" belonged to the people's capacity to receive or to God's capacity to give. Would the blessings rain from heaven until the people had no further room to receive them? (See KJV, NEB.) Or, would they continue until the divine supply was exhausted? I think that the prophet intended to emphasize God's capacity to give, not Israel's capacity to receive. Since His capacity was infinite, His blessings never would cease. In a bold metaphor, the prophet declared that God would bless and bless until no more blessings were left. O blessed impossibility!

Verses 11-12 picture the removal of all obstacles to an abundant harvest in Israel. God promised to destroy the devouring locusts that might threaten the growing crops. He also promised to prevent the vines from shedding their fruit prematurely (v. 11). The Jews' prosperity would be so abundant that all nations would congratulate Israel. Israel would become a land of delight (v. 12). This would be a reversal of the curse that was described in verse 9.

Can we, like Israel, expect to reap rich rewards when we tithe our income? In a sense, for us even to pose such a question is wrong. If our major concern is rewards, we have not discovered the real meaning of Christian stewardship. Giving that is truly Christian is motivated by love—love for God and love for other people. Furthermore, love gives without calculating costs and without expecting rewards. The moment it starts "keeping

*"'I will rebuke the devourer for you, so that it will not destroy the fruits of your soil'"* (Mal. 3:11).

books," it ceases to be love. What was good about the good Samaritan was his unqualified liberality in caring for another person's needs. Jesus also exemplified the principle of self-giving love. For Him, love meant a person's deliberate and uninhibited self-sacrifice in the service of others. From first to last, He lived a life of self-expending service. He walked the second mile, gave everything He had to benefit others, and laid down His life for His friends.

On the other hand, we *do* reap rich rewards when we are faithful stewards of our possessions. Sometimes, these rewards are material in nature, as thousands of Christians can testify. But the greatest rewards are spiritual in nature. They include the joy that comes from knowing that we have helped others. They also include the satisfaction of being able to join hands with other Christians to support our local churches and to reach out through our denomination to minister to a lost world. Above all, our reward consists of knowing that we are partners with God in His great work of redemption. We give because He first gave to us. We love because He first loved us. His unspeakable generosity in giving His Son for us is reason enough for us to want to be generous in our giving to Him.

One of my seminary professors was Olin T. Binkley. In one of his lectures in Christian Ethics, he discussed five ways in which Jesus approved our use of wealth.

1. Jesus taught that to use material resources to meet essential family needs was appropriate. In fact, He condemned the Pharisees for using their gifts to God as an excuse for neglecting their aged parents' needs. (See Mark 7:9-13.) Paul stated the matter: "If any one does not provide for his relatives, and especially for his own family, he has disowned the faith and is worse than an unbeliever" (1 Tim. 5:8).

2. Jesus sanctioned using a portion of our wealth to help the poor. To the rich young ruler, He said: "'Sell all that you have and distribute to the poor, and you will have treasure in heaven; and come, follow me'" (Luke 18:22). Although this was a demand for a specific situation, note the stress on giving to the poor. He cited the good Samaritan as the model for us to follow in relating to our neighbors in need. (See Luke 10:36-37.) He commanded a generous spirit in unforgettable words: "'Give, and it will be given to you; good measure, pressed down,

shaken together, running over, will be put into your lap'" (Luke 6:38*a*).

3. Jesus taught that a portion of our money should be used to support religious institutions. He commended a poor widow for casting two copper coins—all that she had—into the Temple treasury. (See Mark 12:41-44.) Our churches and denominational agencies deserve our support.

4. Jesus recognized that governments have the right to collect taxes and that a part of our income should go for this purpose. When the Pharisees questioned Him about taxes, He responded: "'Render therefore to Caesar the things that are Caesar's, and to God the things that are God's'" (Matt. 22:21).

5. Jesus approved using some of our wealth to add to life's richness and fullness. While He was a guest in a friend's home in Bethany, a woman brought a costly jar of ointment, broke it open, and poured it on His head. When the disciples reproached the woman for what they considered to be waste, Jesus said: "'Let her alone; why do you trouble her? She has done a beautiful thing to me'" (Mark 14:6).

If we were to adopt the disciples' philosophy of life, we would spend our money only to buy life's essentials. We never would "waste" money on life's finer things.

Are you not glad that Jesus indicated His approval for our investing in some things just because they are beautiful? I think He approves when families spend a reasonable amount of their income for travel, entertainment, and recreation. I also think that churches should not feel guilty when they try to make their sanctuaries lovely and conducive to more meaningful worship. Enough drabness is present in the average person's life without our adding to it on Sunday.

According to Dr. Binkley, these were the five categories of spending that Jesus approved. I would add a sixth category. I believe Jesus sanctioned using a portion of our income for savings and investments. In the parable of the talents, He commended the servants who invested wisely and realized good returns on their investments. (See Matt. 25:14-30.) While most of us cannot afford to save a great deal of money, we at least ought to try to make a modest beginning. Persons who save even a modest amount out of each paycheck already have learned to live within their incomes.

## Lessons for Life from Malachi 3:6-12

Let me suggest principles to guide us in stewardship:

*Everything belongs to God.*—We cannot lay claim to any part of it. We brought nothing into the world, and we will take nothing out of it. All we have is a gift from God, and we must answer to Him for the way in which we use His gifts.

*The tithe is a good place to begin in formulating a program of Christian stewardship.*—Tithing promotes regularity in giving, proportionate giving, and skill in money management. Many families discover that the remaining nine-tenths of their incomes seems to go further once they have tithed.

*God does not need to receive our gifts as much as we need to give them (see Ps. 50:9-12), for the essence of life consists of giving rather than receiving.*—To give truly is more blessed than to receive. (See Acts 20:35.)

*Pooling our gifts multiplies their effectiveness.*—When we act in unison, we can accomplish some things that we never could do alone. This is why the Cooperative Program is so important in Southern Baptist life. It enables us to pool our resources in order to mount a major effort in the fields of missions, evangelism, education, and world relief.

*We should follow the rule of never offering to God what costs us nothing. (See 2 Sam. 24:24.)*—God deserves the best that we have to offer, whether talents, time, or money.

*Our gifts are acceptable to God only when they are backed by a life of commitment that is expressed through obedience. (See 1 Sam. 15:22; Isa. 1:11-17.)*—Wicked people's sacrifices are an abomination to the Lord. (See Prov. 15:8; 21:27.) We cannot live for the devil and then expect to bribe God with our gifts.

*While some of tithing's benefits may be material, the greatest blessings are spiritual.*—We will not necessarily have our tithes returned to us with interest, but we will receive many spiritual blessings from God. We will have the joy of knowing that we are partners with Him in the business of living.

*God is looking for dedicated people who can be entrusted with the world's wealth and who will covenant to use it for His glory.*—I know persons who have made this kind of commitment. They have committed themselves to honor God with the profits and material rewards of their businesses, jobs, and professions. They have purposed in their hearts to work diligently to earn all they can, to save all they can, and to give all they can. They have asked God to direct their efforts and have pledged themselves to regard everything they receive as a sacred trust to be used for His glory. Would it not be wonderful if a great host of Christians decided to enter into this kind of partnership with God?

---

1. See the Apocrypha. From *The New English Bible*. Copyright © The Delegates of the Oxford University Press and the Syndics of the Cambridge University Press, 1961, 1970. Reprinted by permission.
2. Ibid., p. 79.
3. Ibid., p. 165.
4. *The Preacher's Task and the Stone of Stumbling* (New York: Harper and Brothers, 1958), p. 114.
5. "Micah—Malachi," *Word Biblical Commentary* (Waco, Texas: Word Books, Publisher, 1984), 32:334.
6. Ibid.

# Personal Learning Activities

1. According to Dr. Page Kelley, Malachi's words about tithing must be set in the larger context of ________________.
   (Choose the correct answer from the list.)
   (1) Worship (3) Repentance
   (2) Economics (4) Culture
2. In 3:7, Malachi charged that the people were guilty of ________________.
3. Malachi also charged that the people were guilty of robbing God of __________ and ______________.
4. According to Dr. Page Kelley, wise use of the earth's resources is not a vital part of our stewardship responsibilities.
   ___True ___False
5. According to Dr. Kelley, the greatest rewards for faithful stewardship are ______________ in nature.

---

Answers: 1. (3); 2. Backsliding; 3. Tithes and offerings; 4. False; 5. Spiritual.

# 6 What Is the Good of Keeping His Charge?



Hebrew Bibles divide Malachi into three chapters rather than four; 4:1-6 appears as 3:19-24. The advantage of this division is that it allows 3:13 to 4:6 to remain intact, as it surely was intended to be. The division of the book into four chapters was patterned after the Septuagint, the Greek version of the Old Testament.

Many parallels exist between the final section of Malachi and the earlier section 2:17 to 3:5. Both mention the harsh manner in which skeptics had spoken against the Lord. (See 2:17; 3:13-15.) Both describe a forerunner's coming to prepare the way before the Lord. (See 3:1; 4:5-6.) Both announce the coming of the great and terrible day of the Lord. (See 3:1-2; 4:1.) Both warn of the fiery judgment that will come on evildoers. (See 3:5; 4:1-3.) Finally, both describe the positive effects of the day of the Lord on the righteous persons. (See 3:3-4,16-18; 4:2.) The contrast between the characters and destinies of the righteous people and of the wicked people is drawn sharply in 3:13 to 4:6.

## Strong Accusations Against God (3:13-15)

The people were hurling strong accusations against God. He charged that their words against Him had been "stout" (v. 13). *The New English Bible* calls them "hard words."[1] The *Good*

*News Bible* comes closest to catching the force of the Hebrew text: "You have said terrible things about me."[2]

The word Malachi used to describe the people's action is the one that was used of Pharaoh when he hardened his heart against the Lord. (See Ex. 7:13,22; 9:35.) The term denotes stubborn resistance to God's will. The people had openly rebelled. They were following the example of their ancestors who had spoken against God in the wilderness.

Oblivious to any wrongdoing on their part, the people demanded: "'How have we spoken against thee?'" From their point of view, they were innocent of all charges against them. Persons in rebellion against God often are likely to regard God as the offender and themselves as the victims. Sin dulls people's consciences and blurs their vision.

Malachi used a form of the Hebrew verb **to speak** that means *to speak to one another*. This suggests that the people's words were not spoken directly to the Lord. They simply gathered in groups and criticized the Lord to one another. However, what people say *about* the Lord can be just as offensive as what they say *to* the Lord. One may take the Lord's name in vain without actually engaging in profanity.

Malachi's listeners had taken the Lord's name in vain. They had questioned the advantage of remaining loyal to God when to them, He seemed to reward evildoers. Three times, Malachi had accused the people of offending God with their speech (see 1:7,12; 2:17; 3:13-15); and each time, the offense grew more serious. They had moved from questioning God (1:7), to wearying Him with their words (2:17), to assailing Him as being unjust (3:13-15). The skillful use of these three accusations helped the prophet move to a climax in developing the thought and substance of his book.

The people's complaints are given in full in verses 14-15. They accused God of crowning the greedy people and crushing the needy persons. They said: "'"It is vain to serve God. What is the good of our keeping his charge or of walking in mourning before the Lord of hosts"'" (v. 14)?

Clearly, the distinctive note of the people's religion had become negative. They thought that the proper way to show one's loyalty to God was by abstinence rather than by action. They approached God in a mournful way with false humility and then reproached Him for failing to reward them. A close similarity can be seen between their attitude and the attitude reflected in Isaiah 58:3; "'"Why have we fasted, and thou seest it not? Why have we humbled ourselves, and thou takest no knowledge of it?"'" The moment we start complaining to God about His failure to take account of the "sacrifices" that we make for Him, we have taken the wrong path. God's true servants do not complain about the sacrifices they make; instead, they rejoice in the spiritual rewards that are theirs.

The people's question in verse 14 might be translated: *What profit is it to us that we have kept his commands?* Their religious motives had become selfish and mercenary. They were serving God solely because they expected to receive something in return. One of the problems with which Malachi had to deal was the widespread notion that God dispensed rewards and punishments strictly on a merit scale. Today, this concept pictures the universe as a giant vending machine. The amount of "goodies" one receives depends on how many coins one drops in. Since Malachi's people had no place in their religion for love-inspired service, they also had no place in it for divine grace.

Verse 15 seems to be the people's deliberate response to the Lord's words in 3:10-12. In the earlier passage, the Lord had challenged them to put Him to the test to see if He would not open the widows of heaven and bless them in an unlimited way. Their response was that evildoers put Him to the test constantly, and yet He did nothing about it (v. 15*b*). Earlier, God had promised that all nations would rise up and call His people blessed (3:12). Their sullen response was that the evildoers were the ones who really were blessed.

D. R. Jones has noted that the prophet's listeners were not merely observing life's injustices, but they actually were recommending those injustices as necessary if one would experience the good life. They had formulated their own set of "beautitudes" that began:

> Blessed are the arrogant and godless;
> Blessed are the evildoers, for they prosper;
> Blessed are those who put God to the test,
> for they escape all punishment.[3]

# God's Faithful Remnant (3:16-17)

Just as a faithful remnant had existed in the days of Elijah (see 1 Kings 19:18), even so some faithful men and women who lived in Malachi's age still loved and feared the Lord. They were the Israel within Israel, the faithful remnant through whom God's will and purpose ultimately would be realized. No doubt, Malachi actively took part in this remnant's work, and his lot was to serve as their spokesman.

While skeptics met together to criticize the Lord (see 2:17; 3:13-15), faithful believers also met. But the believers had a different purpose for meeting. They came together to speak to one another about the Lord's goodness and to reassure one another with words of faith and trust (v. 16). Their attitude, reflected in their conduct, was opposed to the skeptics' attitude. I like to

*"Then those who feared the Lord spoke with one another" (Mal. 3:16).*

think that Malachi must have taken an active part in these praise and testimony meetings.

The Lord did not let the faithful people's words go unnoticed. He heard them; and although He did not act immediately to answer their prayers and to correct earth's injustices, He kept a careful record of their names—and, I believe, of their prayers (v. 16). A book of remembrance was written before Him to preserve this record.

The heavenly book of remembrance reminds us of the ancient kings' custom. They recorded public benefactors' names so that these might be given proper recognition. (See Esther 2:19-23; 6:1-11.) This is not the only Old Testament reference to a record being kept in heaven. (See Ex. 32:32-33; Pss. 56:8; Isa. 4:3; Ezek. 13:9; Dan. 7:10.) The book of remembrance (Mal. 3:16) may have been the forerunner of the book of life mentioned in Revelation 13:8; 20:12.

I think one important lesson we may draw from Malachi 3:16 is that God knows when we are concerned about a difficult situation, even when the most we can do about it is to pray. He hears and takes note of our prayers, even when the answers to them must be delayed. He also is a silent witness to our conversations, and He takes special delight when His people meet together to talk about His goodness. This may not seem like much of a contribution to a difficult situation; but in God's eyes, it is of great worth.

The glorious future reserved for the faithful remnant is set forth in verse 17. They were to occupy a place of honor before the Lord on the approaching day of judgment. They would become His "'special possession.'"

"Special possession" appears in the *Good News Bible* as "my very own" and in the *New International Version* as "my treasured possession."[4] These are attempts to translate a Hebrew word that occurs only eight times in the Old Testament. Twice, it is used with reference to a king's private treasure. Because of his devotion to God's house, David contributed his entire private treasure of silver and gold for its construction. (See 1 Chron. 29:3-5.) According to Ecclesiastes 2:8, another king's private treasure included stores of silver and gold.

G. A. F. Knight has described the basic significance of the unusual Hebrew word beautifully:

> In olden days a king was the ultimate owner of everything in the land he ruled. He owned every building, every farm, every coin. But that kind of "owning" could give him little personal satisfaction. Consequently in his palace he kept a treasure chest of his "very own," in which he delighted to store the precious stones and *objets d'art* which he loved to handle. This treasure-box was his *segullah* [the Hebrew word for "special possession," writer's explanation]. In the same way, God, who made the whole earth, and to whom all nations belonged, looked now upon Israel as his own peculiar treasure.[5]

Six times, the Hebrew word is applied to the Israelites as the Lord's "private treasure" or "special possession." The first occurrence is in Exodus 19:5: "Now therefore, if you will obey my voice and keep my covenant, you shall be my own possession among all peoples; for all the earth is mine." Deuteronomy has the term three times, translating it as "a people for his own possession" (Deut. 7:6; 14:2; 26:18). In addition to the use of this term in Malachi, a similar usage occurs in Psalm 135:4: "For the Lord has chosen Jacob for himself, Israel as his own possession."

The word translated "special possession" (Mal. 3:17) also found its way into the New Testament through the influence of the Septuagint (Greek) translation of the Old Testament. There, it describes the rich inheritance that belongs to Christians (Eph. 1:14) and the unique relationship that exists between them and their Lord (Titus 2:14; 1 Peter 2:9). God always puts supreme value on persons and considers those who are joined to Him as His highest treasure. This is set forth even more forcibly in the King James Version's translation of Malachi 3:17: "And they shall be mine, saith the Lord of hosts, in that day when I make up my jewels."

God's highest concern is with His people's spiritual welfare. Any church that does not place people's welfare as its highest priority has failed to follow His example.

God further promised that He would spare the faithful remnant, just as a father might spare his son who served him faithfully (3:17*b*). **To spare** also means *to have compassion* or *to* *take pity*. It usually has as its object one who is threatened by imminent danger and is unable to deliver himself/herself. The noun derived from this verb is used in Isaiah 63:9 to describe the Lord's tender concern for His afflicted people: "In all their affliction he was afflicted, and the angel of his presence saved them; in his love and in his pity he redeemed them; he lifted them up and carried them all the days of old." James Hastings has noted the Book of Malachi teaches that God spares the righteous "not as a judge spares a stranger, whom he dismisses from his bar, but as a father spares a son, whom he takes to his bosom. . . . Not as David would have spared Absalom, but as Abraham would have spared Isaac."[6]

## The Destinies of the Righteous and of the Wicked (3:18 to 4:3)

Malachi 3:18 to 4:3 contrasts the righteous people's character and destiny to the wicked people's character and destiny. The righteous people have no cause to fear the day of the Lord, for it will bring them healing and renewed vigor (4:2). On the other hand, the wicked people will be consumed in the fires of judgment (4:1) and will become ashes under the righteous people's feet (4:3). The Bible indicates in no uncertain terms the grim fate that awaits those who set themselves against the Lord and reject His offer of salvation and forgiveness.

Verse 18 is Malachi's response to the criticisms made against the Lord in 2:17; 3:14-15. There, skeptics had charged that whether one was righteous or wicked made little difference, since the Lord did not seem to distinguish between the two. If anything, He seemed to favor the wicked people.

The prophet responded that on the day of the Lord, the people "once more" would be able to distinguish between the righteous and the wicked, between those who served God and those who did not serve Him (v. 18). "Once more" probably refers to the superior spiritual insight of their ancestors.

The contrast between the righteous people's destiny and the wicked people's destiny is brought into sharp focus in 4:1-3. George Adam Smith described this contrast vividly:

> The Apocalypse of this last judgment is one of the grandest. To the wicked it shall be a fire, root and branch shall they be burned out, but to the righteous a fair morning of God, as when dawn comes to those who have been sick and sleepless through the night, and its beams bring healing, even as to the popular belief of Israel it was the rays of the morning sun which distilled the dew. They break into life and energy, like calves leaping from the dark pen into the sunshine. To this morning landscape a grim figure is added. They shall tread down the wicked and arrogant like ashes.[7]

"'For behold, the day comes, burning like an oven, when all the arrogant and all evildoers will be stubble; the day that comes shall burn them up, says the Lord of hosts, so that it will leave them neither root nor branch'" (4:1).

T. V. Moore has described the judgment's severity:

> All previous judgments are but reddenings of the dawn, that betokened the coming, but did not unfold the terrible brightness of that awful day. . . . There is something very forceful in these abrupt exclamations, as if the prophet was elevated on some mount of vision, and actually beheld this terrible pomp come rolling up the distant skies, on its reddening pathway of fire and blood.[8]

The word "behold" is used four times in Malachi to introduce divine proclamations (2:3; 3:1; 4:1,5). It makes the proclamations more emphatic. Malachi did not doubt the nearness of the day of judgment and the certainty of its coming.

Malachi compared the day to an oven in which the wicked would be consumed. The word for **oven** is ***tannur,*** a word that indicates *a clay oven or fire-pot*. W. E. Barnes has described the modern counterpart to these ancient ovens:

> The same name . . . is applied in modern Palestine to the ovens in which bread is made. A large hole is made in the earth, the sides are plastered, a very fierce fire is made at the bottom with grass or thorns or twigs ("stubble"), and after the removal of the embers flat cakes of bread are stuck against the plastered sides and very quickly cooked.[9]

Malachi continued the metaphor of the oven by comparing the wicked people with the grass and the stubble with which the oven was fired. Jesus used the same metaphor when He spoke of the grass of the field "which today is alive and tomorrow is thrown into the oven" (Matt. 6:30). Evildoers would be destroyed so completely that neither root nor branch would be left to them.

The metaphor changes in verse 2. Malachi moved from the oven's searing heat to the morning sun's gentle rays. The prophet promised that for those who feared the Lord, the sun of righteousness would rise with healing in its wings. To fear the Lord does not mean to cringe before Him in fear as a criminal might cringe before a judge. Rather, it means to reverence and respect Him, and to turn away from sin. From a Christian standpoint, this means letting Christ be Savior and Lord of our lives.

The sun's "wings" are its shining rays. In the ancient world, the sun was a common symbol of blessing and protection. It often was represented as a winged disk beaming its blessings on the earth below. However, because of the prevalence of sun worship among the Gentiles the Jews were reluctant to apply sun imagery to God lest it be misunderstood. The one exception to the rule of not applying sun imagery to God seems to be Psalm 84:11: "For the Lord God is a sun and shield; he bestows favor and honor. No good thing does the Lord withhold from those who walk uprightly."

Malachi's use of sun imagery also may have been influenced by Isaiah 60:1-3, which declares that the light of God's glory would dawn on His people to dispel their darkness and to banish their sorrow and suffering. Although the Isaiah passage does not contain the word "sun," it clearly conveys the notion that the Lord is like the sun.

"Sun of righteousness" (Mal. 4:2) is not to be taken as a personification of God but as a figure that represents righteousness. Malachi foretold a time when righteousness, understood as vindication and victory, would flood the lives of God's people as the sun floods the earth with its light.

Throughout the ages, Christians have proclaimed the fulfillment of Malachi's hope in Jesus Christ. He came as God's "dayspring from on high" (Luke 1:78, KJV), sent that those who sit in darkness and the shadow of death might have light. Paul expressed this idea vividly: "For it is the God who said, 'Let light shine out of darkness,' who has shone in our hearts to give the light of the knowledge of the glory of God in the face of Christ" (2 Cor. 4:6).

The response of the righteous people to the healing sunlight is compared with the response of calves who are let out of the stall. It is a picture of leaping and bounding as the calves enjoy their newfound freedom. To find a more appropriate description of the exuberance of a life that is liberated from sin and death would be difficult. None but God's loved ones know the fullness of joy that He gives.

Verse 3 reverts to the imagery of verse 1, where Malachi indicated that on the day of the Lord the wicked will be reduced to ashes. Verse 3 adds that on that great and terrible day, the righteous people will go forth and trample on the wicked people's ashes. This is heightened prophetic speech, and we must not impose a literal interpretation on it. Its basic meaning is that righteousness alone endures and that evil carries within it the seeds of its own destruction.

## Concluding Admonitions and Warnings (4:4-6)

That Moses and Elijah appear together in the closing verses of the last prophetic book is hardly by accident. The next time these two appeared together was at the mount of transfiguration when they met with the Savior and talked of His coming death in Jerusalem. (See Luke 9:28-31.)

Verse 4, with its admonition for the people to remember the law of Moses, serves as a conclusion not only to the Book of Malachi but also to the entire collection of prophetic writings. The ancient Hebrews designated as "the Prophets" not only Isaiah, Jeremiah, Ezekiel, and the Twelve Minor Prophets (which they called "the Latter Prophets"), but also the Books of Joshua, Judges, 1 and 2 Samuel, and 1 and 2 Kings (which they called "the Former Prophets"). Once we realize that for them the canon of the prophets extended from Joshua to Malachi, the exhortation at the end of Malachi to remember the law of Moses takes on added significance. A similar admonition is at the beginning of Joshua (Josh. 1:1,8). From first to last, the prophets magnified the law and called the people to observe it.

Thus, the Old Testament testifies to the inseparable link between the law and the prophets. Law was regarded as the basis of Israel's existence, and prophecy applied law to daily living. Through prophecy, the law was made effective. Thus, the exhortation to remember the law of Moses was not a legalistic afterthought. It expressed a conviction of the law's importance that lay at the heart of the Old Testament. A. F. Kirkpatrick answered those who see law and prophecy as opposed.

> There was no antagonism between the law and the prophets; and it was not unworthy of the latest voice of prophecy that it should bid Israel put its conscience to school with the law, during the centuries in which the voice of prophecy was to be silent, and a life and death conflict was to be waged with heathenism.
>
> It was the lesson needed for the age; and if Israel misused the law, and forged fetters for itself out of what God designed for its support, the fault lay in them, and not in the prophet.[10]

The Hebrew verb translated "to remember" carried the idea of acting on what was remembered. Thus, to remember the law of Moses meant to live in accord with its demands. In Old Testament thought, true remembrance could not be separated from obedience. (See Ex. 20:8; Num. 15:40.) How would this principle affect us if we applied it to our observance of the Lord's Supper, our "remembering" His death for us?

If verse 4 looks to the past and calls for remembrance, verses 5-6 look to the future and call for watchfulness. These verses carry the thought of 3:1-5, where the Lord's coming is preceded by His messenger's coming. In the closing epilogue (vv. 5-6), the mysterious messenger is identified with the prophet Elijah. Elijah was well-suited for this role because of his pioneer work as a prophet and because he had been taken up to heaven in a chariot of fire (or whirlwind; see 2 Kings 2:11-12). Because of Malachi 4:5-6, Elijah came to play a vital role in later apocalyptic thought. (See Wisdom of Sirach 48:1-14; see also Mark 9:11-13; Luke 1:17.)

Malachi described Elijah's mission as turning the fathers' hearts to their children and the children's hearts to their fathers (v. 6). The most natural interpretation of this verse regards the "fathers" as the Jewish people's godly ancestors and the "children" as the prophet's contemporaries. Because of their evildoing, the children needed to be restored to the faith of their fathers. A reconciling of the generations, a healing of the "generation gap," needed to take place.

Elijah was thought to be the person most likely to bring reconciliation about, since once before he had succeeded in turning the people's hearts back to God. (See 1 Kings 18:37.) Commenting on Elijah's mission, George Adam Smith wrote:

> This is the confession of Prophecy that the number of her servants is exhausted and her message to Israel fulfilled. She can do no more for the people than she has done. But she will summon up her old energy and fire in the return of her strongest personality and make one great effort to convert the nation before the Lord strike them with judgement.[11]

If Elijah failed in his mission—and the book ends on this somber note—the Lord would come and smite the land with a curse. The word translated **curse** is ***cherem,*** a word that was applied to certain objects which, because of their unholy character, the Lord commanded to be destroyed completely and ruthlessly. The word gained special significance during the period of the conquest when it was applied to the Canaanite cities and their goods that were destined for destruction. E. W. Hengstenberg noted that Israel obtained possession of Canaan as the holy God's holy people and simply had to choose between *holiness* and ***cherem.*** "If Israel became Canaan in heart, it would also become Canaan in its fate."[12]

Since John the Baptist fulfilled the prophecy of Elijah's coming, some interesting questions arise. Did he succeed in turning the people's hearts back to the faith of their fathers? If not, was the land of Israel smitten with a curse? Was this perhaps related to the Romans destroying Jerusalem in AD 70? Does this constitute a warning to Baptists as we consider the seriousness of God's call to repentance?

Quite appropriately, the Book of Malachi has been placed at

the end of the prophets. With its announcement of the forerunner, the Lord's coming, the day of judgment, and the righteous people's future blessedness, it serves as a bridge that links the Old Testament with the New Testament. With its uncompromising demand for religious faith, moral integrity, and social justice, it challenges us to a deeper commitment to the faith of our fathers. If we truly are concerned with rekindling the fires of faith in our generation, we will give serious attention to Malachi's message.

# Lessons for Life from Malachi 3:13 to 4:6

*People in rebellion against God are likely to regard God as the offender and themselves as innocent victims.*—Sin dulls people's consciences and blurs their vision.

*One may take the Lord's name in vain without actually engaging in profanity.*—One who always is complaining and criticizing God for the way He manages affairs is guilty of this sin. One who whines and complains never makes a good witness and may have the opposite effect. Are people drawn to the Lord by the positive nature of our witness?

*God does not dispense rewards and punishments strictly on the basis of the merits we earn.*—A works-righteousness leaves no room either for unselfish service or for divine grace. God's forgiveness always is a gift of free grace, and our service to Him should be motivated by a love that demands nothing in return.

*God always has a faithful remnant of believers who can be counted on to stand firm even when others forsake Him.*—Seven thousand people in Elijah's day had not bowed their knees to Baal. (See 1 Kings 19:18.) In Jesus' day, faithful men and women like Simeon and Anna devoted themselves to prayer and looked "for the consolation of Israel" (Luke 2:25-26,36-37). God still has His faithful remnant in our time. Are we part of the Master's minority?

*God notices our prayers, our words of praise and testimony, and even our unspoken yearnings.*—They all are written in His book of remembrance. He always remembers those who are His, and He has promised never to leave or forsake them.

*A grim fate awaits those who persist in their rebellion against God.*—They may get by with their rebellion for awhile—and even seem to prosper in it—but the Bible teaches that a day of judgment is coming. Then the evil people will be destroyed like dry stubble in a hot oven.

*God's people have no need to fear judgment, for it only will bring them healing, reward, and renewed strength.*—For them, it will be a time of exuberant joy, as when calves are let loose from a cramped stall. Then let the singing and shouting begin! A great day is coming for God's people!

---

1. From *The New English Bible*. Copyright © The Delegates of the Oxford University Press and the Syndics of the Cambridge University Press, 1961, 1970. Reprinted by permission.
2. This quotation is from the *Good News Bible*, the Bible in Today's English Version. Old Testament: Copyright © American Bible Society 1976; New Testament: Copyright © American Bible Society 1966, 1971, 1976. Used by permission. Subsequent quotations are marked GNB.
3. "Haggai, Zechariah and Malachi," *Torch Bible Commentary* (London: SCM Press, Ltd., 1962), p. 203.
4. HOLY BIBLE *New International Version*, copyright © 1978, New York Bible Society. Used by permission.
5. *Law and Grace* (Philadelphia: Westminster Press, 1962), p. 25.
6. *The Great Texts of the Bible*, (New York: Charles Scribner's Sons, 1915), 2:500-501.
7. *The Book of the Twelve Prophets*, New and Revised Edition (New York: Doubleday, Doran & Company Inc., 1929), 2:362-363.
8. *Prophets of the Restoration* (New York: Robert Carter and Brothers, 1856), p. 399.
9. *'Haggai, Zechariah, and Malachi,' The Cambridge Bible Series* (Cambridge: Cambridge University Press, 1917), p. 22.
10. *The Doctrine of the Prophets* (Grand Rapids, Mich.: Zondervan Pub. House, 1958), p. 508.
11. Smith, *The Twelve Prophets*, 2:365.
12. *Christology of the Old Testament* 2nd edition, trans. James Martin (Edinburgh: T. and T. Clark, 1865), 4:230.

# Personal Learning Activities

1. When God charged His people with speaking "stout" words against Him, He meant that they (select the proper response from the list):

___(1) Used profanity ___(3) Spoke hastily
___(2) Took His name in vain ___(4) Argued strongly

2. What two blessings did God's faithful remnant receive?
3. Malachi compared the day of judgment with __________.
   (Choose the correct answer from the list.)
   (1) An oven (3) A flood
   (2) A storm (4) A famine
4. Malachi concluded his book by exhorting his people to remember and to heed his words (4:4). ___True ___False
5. In 4:5-6, the prophet announced God's promise that He would send ________________ before the day of the Lord came. (Select the correct answer from the list.)
   (1) David (3) Elijah
   (2) Jeremiah (4) Isaiah

Answers: 1. (2); 2. Their names were written in God's book of remembrance; they would be spared; 3. (1); 4. False; 5. (3)

# The Church Study Course

The Church Study Course consists of a variety of short-term credit courses for adults and youth and noncredit foundational units for children and preschoolers. The materials are for use in addition to the study and training curriculums made available to the churches on an ongoing basis.

Study courses and foundational units are organized into a system that is promoted by the Sunday School Board, 127 Ninth Avenue, North, Nashville, Tennessee 37234; by the Woman's Missionary Union, Highway 280, East, 100 Missionary Ridge, Birmingham, Alabama 35243-2798; by the Brotherhood Commission, 1548 Poplar Avenue, Memphis, Tennessee 38104; and by the respective departments of the state conventions affiliated with the Southern Baptist Convention.

Study course materials are flexible enough to be adapted to the needs of any Baptist church. The resources are published in several different formats—textbooks of various sizes, workbooks, and kits. Each item contains a brief explanation of the Church Study Course and information on requesting credit. Additional information and interpretation are available from the participating agencies.

**Types of Study and Credit**

Adults and youth can earn study course credit through individual or group study. Teachers of courses or of foundational units also are eligible to receive credit.

1. Class Experience.—Group involvement with course material for the designated number of hours for the particular course and reading the textbook. A person who is absent from one or more sessions must complete the "Personal Learning Activities" or other requirements for the course.
2. Individual Study.—Reading, viewing, or listening to course material and completing the specified requirements for the course.

3. Lesson Course Study.—Parallel use of designated study course material during the study of selected units in Church Program Organization periodical curriculum units. Guidance for this means of credit is in the selected periodical.
4. Institutional Study.—Parallel use of designated study course material during regular courses at educational institutions, including Seminary Extension Department courses. Guidance for this means of credit is provided by the teacher.

Credit is awarded for the successful completion of a course of study. This credit is granted by the Church Study Course Awards Office, 127 Ninth Avenue, North, Nashville, Tennessee 37234, for the participating agencies. Form 725 (available free) is recommended for use in requesting credit.

A permanent record of courses and diplomas will be maintained by the Awards Office. Twice each year, up-to-date reports called "transcripts" will be sent to churches to distribute to members who take part in the Church Study Course. Each transcript will list courses and diplomas that participants have completed and will show progress toward diplomas that are being sought. The transcript will show which courses are needed to complete diploma requirements. A diploma will be issued automatically when the final requirement is met.

Detailed information about the Church Study Course system of credits, diplomas, and record keeping is available from the participating agencies. Study course materials, supplementary teaching or learning aids, and forms for record keeping may be ordered from Baptist Book Stores.

**The Church Study Course Curriculum**

Credit is granted on those courses listed in the current copy of the *Church Services and Materials Catalog* and the *Church Study Course Catalog*. When selecting courses or foundational units, check the current catalogs to determine what study course materials are valid.

# How to Request Credit for This Course

This book is designed for a course in the subject area Bible Studies.

This course is designed for 5 hours of group study. Credit is awarded for satisfactory class experience with the study material for the minimum number of hours which includes reading the textbook. A person who is absent from one or more sessions must complete the "Personal Learning Activities" or other requirements for the materials missed.

Credit also is allowed for use of this material in individual study and in institutional study, if so designated.

The following requirements must be met for credit:

1. Read the book *Malachi: Rekindling the Fires of Faith*.
2. Attend at least 5 hours of class study or complete all "Personal Learning Activities" (see end of each chapter). Class members who are absent from one or more class sessions must complete "Personal Learning Activities" on chapters missed. In such a case, they must turn in their papers by the date the teacher sets, usually within ten days following the last class.

Credit in this course may be earned through individual study. The requirements for such credit are:

1. Read the book.
2. Complete the "Personal Learning Activities" on the chapters.

Credit in this course may be earned through study in an educational institution, if so designated by a teacher. The requirements are:

1. Read the book.
2. Fulfill the requirements of the course taught at the institution.

After the course is completed, the teacher, the study course records librarian, the learner, or any person designated by the church should complete Form 725 ("Church Study Course Enrollment/Credit Request") and send it to the Awards Office, 127 Ninth Avenue, North, Nashville, Tennessee 37234. In the back of this book the reader will find a form which may be cut out, filled in, and sent to the Awards Office.

## CHURCH STUDY COURSE
## ENROLLMENT/CREDIT REQUEST (FORM-725)

PERSONAL CSC NUMBER (If Known)

INSTRUCTIONS:
1. Please PRINT or TYPE.
2. COURSE CREDIT REQUEST—Requirements must be met. Use exact title.
3. ENROLLMENT IN DIPLOMA PLANS—Enter selected diploma title to enroll.
4. For additional information see the Church Study Course Catalog.
5. Duplicate additional forms as needed. Free forms are available from the Awards Office and State Conventions.

TYPE OF REQUEST: (Check all that apply)

☐ Course Credit
☐ Enrollment in Diploma Plan
☐ Address Change
☐ Name Change
☐ Church Change

CHURCH
- Church Name
- Mailing Address
- City, State, Zip Code

REQUEST FOR
- ☐ Mr. ☐ Mrs. ☐ Miss ☐
- DATE OF BIRTH → Month | Day | Year
- Name (First, Mi, Last)
- Street, Route, or P.O. Box
- City, State, Zip Code

### COURSE CREDIT REQUEST

| Course No. | Use exact title |
|---|---|
| | 1. Malachi: Rekindling the Fires of Faith |
| | 2. |
| | 3. |
| | 4. |
| | 5. |

### ENROLLMENT IN DIPLOMA PLANS

If you have not previously indicated a diploma(s) you wish to earn, or you are beginning work on a new one(s), select and enter the diploma title from the current Church Study Course Catalog. Select one that relates to your leadership responsibility or interest. When all requirements have been met, the diploma will be automatically mailed to your church. No charge will be made for enrollment or diplomas.

| Title of diploma | Age group or area |
|---|---|
| 1. | |
| 2. | |

Signature of Pastor, Teacher, or Study Leader | Date

MAIL THIS REQUEST TO → CHURCH STUDY COURSE AWARDS OFFICE
RESEARCH SERVICES DEPARTMENT
127 NINTH AVENUE, NORTH
NASHVILLE, TENNESSEE 37234

FORM-725 (Rev. 7-83)

Read Acts 15 + 2+3